RISE™

Identity & Worth

RISE

Rooted ❖ Intentional ❖ Strong ❖ Energized™

A transformational book series

exploring balance, belief, and embodied wholeness.

RISE™

Identity & Worth

Living a

Rooted, Intentional, Strong, and Energized Life™

Volume 1

Angel Tate Keaton

Healthy in Heart Media™, LLC
Roanoke, VA

Published in the United States of America by
Healthy in Heart Media™, LLC
P.O. Box 694
Vinton, VA 24179
Copyright © 2026 by Angel Tate Keaton
First Printing January 2026
Cover art and design by the author

Library of Congress Control Number: 2026900229

ISBN— 978-1-969064-18-0

Trademark Notice

RISE Rooted, Intentional, Strong, Energized™, and related marks and program names are trademarks of Healthy in Heart Media, LLC. Unauthorized use is prohibited.

Disclaimer

The author of this book does not dispense medical advice or prescribe the use of any technique as a form of treatment for medical, emotional, psychological, or physical conditions without the guidance of a licensed physician or qualified healthcare provider, either directly or indirectly. The intent of the author is solely to offer information of a general nature to support you in your personal journey toward emotional, physical, mental, and spiritual well-being.

If you choose to apply any of the information presented in this book, you do so of your own volition. The author and the publisher assume no responsibility for your actions or any consequences that may arise from the use or misuse of the information contained herein.

No Guarantee of Outcomes
The practices and concepts presented in this book are intended to support whole-being wellness. Individual experiences and results may vary. The author and publisher make no guarantees regarding any specific physical, emotional, or spiritual outcomes resulting from the application of this material.

Educational Purpose Notice
This book is provided for general informational and educational purposes only and is not intended as a substitute for professional medical, psychological, counseling, or therapeutic care.

Emergency Help Notice
This material is not intended for crises. If you are experiencing a medical, mental-health, or safety emergency, contact local emergency services or a licensed professional immediately.

No Professional Relationship Notice
Reading this book does not establish a counseling, coaching, therapeutic, or professional relationship between the reader and the author or publisher. This material is for personal growth and educational use only and is not a substitute for individualized professional advice, diagnosis, or treatment.

Spiritual Disclaimer
Spiritual references and practices presented in this book reflect the author's personal faith and are offered for reflection, not as doctrinal instruction or religious authority.

Scripture Notice
Unless otherwise noted, all Scripture quotations are taken from the American Standard Version (ASV), as provided by BibleGateway.com. The American Standard Version was originally published in 1901 and is now in the public domain. This version was chosen for its consistent use of the divine name in the Old Testament and its closer alignment with the original Hebrew, making it a suitable foundation for a return-to-Eden perspective.

Dedication

For the brave women of the RISE Momentum Circle—
You are proof that healing multiplies when shared.

Thank you for showing up.
For daring to believe healing is possible.
For choosing restoration over resignation.
For rising again and again.

Your courage is the heartbeat of this work.
May you continue to stand rooted, intentional, strong, and energized—
and never forget that your life is worth rising for.

Rise each day like the sun—

Rooted in truth,

Intentional in habits,

Strong in spirit, and

Energized for the hope of tomorrow.

~Angel Tate Keaton

When the phoenix burns,
It does not perish.
It rises from the ashes—refined.

Table of Contents

Preface — Why I Wrote This Book

I didn't write this book because I had life figured out.
I wrote it because my life fell apart.

There was a time when getting through each day felt like walking through mud —
the kind that clings to your feet and makes every step heavy. I kept trying to push
harder, do better, pray more, look happier… anything to quiet the ache inside me
that kept whispering:

This is not the life you were made for.

I tried to fix myself with diets, devotionals, and determination.
I measured my worth by my weight, my productivity, and my ability to hide the
parts of me I thought were "too much." I made myself small, hoping to feel
acceptable, but shrinking only made the emptiness louder.

Eventually, my body, mind, and spirit all said "no more."
Illness shook me awake.
Faith kept me from giving up.
And a gentle nudge from God led me toward something I had never truly
considered:

Healing.

Not the kind that comes in a pill bottle or an overnight miracle…
but the kind that grows slowly, like roots finding the soil again.

RISE™ began there —
at the intersection of exhaustion and hope.

It became my permission slip to live differently:
to nourish instead of punish,
to listen instead of hustle,
to befriend instead of battling my own body.

I never planned to write a book about whole-being wellness. Honestly, I was just trying to get through the day.

For years, I checked every box I thought would make me "better" — better Christian, better mother, better body, better everything. But the harder I tried, the more disconnected I became. My body was struggling, my emotions were buried, and my spirit was running on fumes.

Eventually, I had to face the questions I'd been avoiding:

What if I don't need to be "better?"
What if what I really need is to be *whole?*

Those questions changed my life.

I started learning — slowly and stubbornly — how to care for all of me:
• my physical health without obsession
• my emotions without shame
• my faith without fear
• my identity without conditions

That's where RISE took shape.

RISE is not a diet, a doctrine, or a checklist.
It's a framework for living rooted in who you are, not who you're trying to prove yourself to be.

And as I learned to rise, I couldn't keep that rise to myself.

This book is the first step of an invitation — back to rhythm, back to peace, back to the truth that you were created for a fully alive life.

You don't have to earn that life.
You only have to return to it.

So, if you feel tired… welcome.
If you feel lost… welcome.
If something inside you knows there must be more than this…whatever this looks like for you… welcome.

You are already on the path.
Let's walk it together.

Welcome to RISE: a journey back to the wholeness that has always been yours. You were created for a life that feels nourishing, not depleting.

This book is a beginning — your beginning of balance, your return to wholeness.

Take your time.
Take a breath.
Take what helps and leave the rest.

Let's rise into that life — together.

Acknowledgments

To the women of the RISE Momentum Circle—
you are the heartbeat of this message and the inspiration behind every page.
Thank you for trusting me, challenging me,
and walking this journey toward wholeness together.

To my husband, Todd—
thank you for believing in me long before I believed in myself.
Your patience, steady love, and gentle strength lift me higher.

To those who poured truth into me—teachers, mentors, and healers—
thank you for pointing me toward freedom when fear tried to claim the final word.

And to every person who ever whispered hope into my healing—I carry your words
in these pages.

Most of all, to my Creator—thank You for breath, for belonging, and for the
balance You designed from the beginning.
May this work honor You.

With profound gratitude,
Angel Tate Keaton

How to Use This Book

This book is designed to support your whole-being wellness — body, mind, emotions, and spirit — one week at a time. There is no rush, no falling behind, and no "right" way to move through it. There is only your pace and your presence.

This is a guided journey, not a demand. Let it meet you where you are.

Your Personal Journey

Most readers will walk this path individually, using the weekly rhythm as a steady companion for reflection, renewal, and gentle forward movement. Even when you are reading alone, you are not isolated. Many others are engaging these same pillars, asking similar questions, and learning to listen to their inner wisdom alongside you.

This book is meant to be a safe place to think, feel, and grow — without performance or pressure.

Optional Guided Connection

If you are interested in participating in an author-led RISE Momentum Circle, you may request more information directly. These guided spaces, when available, are facilitated by the creator of this work and are designed to remain grounded, trauma-informed, and rooted in encouragement rather than instruction or therapy.

Participation is always optional, and availability may vary. This book is complete and supportive as a standalone journey.

If you'd like to explore current or future RISE Momentum Circle offerings, you can visit: healthyinheart.com/contact-me-about-r-i-s-e

Your Weekly Rhythm in This Book

Each week centers on one pillar of RISE and includes:

1. **A short chapter** — offering perspective, meaning, and practical wisdom
2. **Reflection prompts** — questions that help turn insight into lived awareness
3. **One focus practice** — a small, doable step to embody what you are learning

4. **RISE Check-In** — space to notice what is growing, shifting, or asking for care

Simple. Steady. Sustainable.

Pairing With the RISE Journal

This book is part of the *RISE*^{TM} *Circle of Wholeness Collection.*

The **RISE™ Identity & Worth Journal: A 12 Week Journey to a Rooted, Intentional, Strong, and Energized Life** is a companion resource that supports daily integration. It includes:

- daily reflection spaces
- breath and body-awareness prompts
- weekly acknowledgments of progress
- visual reminders of ritual, rhythm, and rest

If you are using both, this book offers the **why** — the journal supports the **how**.

A Trauma-Informed Journey

Healing should never feel forced.

Throughout this book, you will find invitations — not requirements. You are always free to:

- skip a prompt
- take more time
- pause when emotions feel big
- return when your heart feels ready

Your nervous system is your guide.
Honor what feels safe, spacious, and supportive.

This journey is about restoration, not endurance.

A Final Word Before We Begin

Wholeness isn't something that happens all at once.
It grows slowly—like becoming *Real*.*

Shaped by honesty, softened by love,
and strengthened every time you choose to stay present
instead of disappearing.

You don't become whole through perfection—
you become whole by being **fully here**:
scuffs, scars, beauty, and all.

So, take a deep breath.
You're not stepping into performance—
you're stepping into presence.
Each small choice, each loving moment,
brings you one step closer to a more
authentic, embodied, beautifully Real **you**.

Welcome to your next rise.
Let's begin

* This reflection is lovingly inspired by the conversation on becoming "Real" from
The Velveteen Rabbit *by Margery Williams (1922).*

Overview of the RISE Framework

A Pathway Back to Whole-Being Wellness

RISE is more than a wellness model—it is a return to the way we were created to live:

Rooted • Intentional • Strong • Energized

Every person rises through four dimensions—body, mind, spirit, and community—each intertwined like threads in a tapestry of wholeness. Before we reshape habits or rebuild rhythms, we begin with identity.

Identity steadies the ground beneath us so change can take root. That is why Identity & Worth Volume 1 introduces the RISE way of living by anchoring you in who you truly are, long before we expand into deeper lifestyle practices in future volumes.

The RISE Framework gives language, symbols, and gentle practices that begin transforming daily life one small, meaningful shift at a time.

R — Rooted

Rooted people are steady, grounded, nourished, and connected.

Circumstances, labels, or storms do not define them, because their identity is anchored in something deeper and more eternal.

To be rooted is to live from truth—not reaction.

Rootedness looks like:

> Strong internal foundations
>
> Eating what nourishes the body
>
> Slowing down enough to listen
>
> Returning to who you are beneath old labels

Choosing connection over chaos

Rooted people grow with confidence because they are not afraid of being uprooted.

I — Intentional

Intentional living means moving through life with clarity, purpose, and conscious choice.

It is the opposite of drifting, numbing, or living from inherited beliefs.

Intentionality expresses itself through:

Mindfulness in daily decisions

Choosing rather than reacting

Creating rhythms instead of chasing urgency

Speaking truth with compassion

Aligning actions with deeply held values

Intentional people move with meaning—even in the smallest moments.

S — Strong

Strength is not force.

It is integrity, emotional steadiness, and inner resilience.

It is the capacity to stay rooted in truth even when life shakes the ground.

RISE strength includes:

Emotional stability

Boundaries that honor self and others

Courage to speak and choose wisely

Resilience in adversity

A balanced confidence

Willingness to heal and grow

Strength allows you to face life with a steady heart and a grounded identity.

E — Energized

Energized living is not a frantic hustle or endless output.

It is sustainable, life-giving vitality—the natural fruit of alignment, nourishment, and inner freedom.

Energized people experience:

Joy that flows without force

Rhythms of work and rest that restore

Clarity instead of overwhelm

Purpose without burnout

A sense of internal lightness

This is what it means to be fully alive.

The Circle of Wholeness

A Whole-System View of Human Flourishing

The Circle of Wholeness is the visual model that holds the entire RISE ecosystem.

It teaches that wellness is not linear—it is circular, interconnected, and dynamic.

In the Circle:

> Every area of life impacts every other

> Small choices ripple outward

> Minor shifts create meaningful healing

You cannot "fix" one area without touching the whole.

The Circle of Wholeness includes Nine Pillars, each represented by a nature-based symbol.

These symbols are simple, universal, and spiritually resonant—giving every participant a way to connect with truth no matter their background.

The Nine Pillars of Wholeness

Each pillar includes its symbol, meaning, practice, and reflection question.

1. The Tree of Life — Rooted Health

Meaning: Connection, nourishment, vitality.

Wholeness begins underground: strong roots create strong lives.

Practice:

> Eat from creation (living foods)
>
> Move with gratitude
>
> Rest before exhaustion

Reflection: What keeps my roots strong today?

2. The Scales of Balance — Living in Alignment

Meaning: Harmony across body, mind, spirit, and relationships.

Balance is alignment, not perfection.

Practice:

Pause midday to breathe and recenter

Simplify one crowded area

Reflection: Where can I recalibrate gently instead of striving?

3. The Radiant Human — Flowing Energy Within

Meaning: Inner light and vitality flow when beliefs, thoughts, and spirit agree.

Practice:

Begin with three deep breaths

Practice prayer, meditation, or mindful movement

Reflection: How can I let my inner light guide my pace?

4. Hands of Stewardship — Nurturing What's Given

Meaning: Responsibility, gratitude, tending what has been entrusted.

Practice:

Do one act of care (body, home, relationship)

Offer encouragement or gratitude

Reflection: What am I stewarding with love today?

5. The Garden Path — Healing as a Journey

Meaning: Healing is not linear; it unfolds over time.

Practice:

Notice progress without judgment

Rest purposefully once a week

Reflection: What is today teaching me about patience?

6. The Water Ripple — The Power of Small Choices

Meaning: Every choice sends ripples into the whole.

Practice:

Make one nourishing choice

Notice its ripple into mood and relationships

Reflection: How can one small shift bring wider peace?

7. The Circle of People — Healing Together

Meaning: We heal in community, not isolation.

Practice:

>Reach out to encourage

>Ask for help when needed

Reflection: Who forms my circle of support?

8. Sunrise Over Mountains — Renewal & Hope

Meaning: Dawn after darkness; every day a new beginning.

Practice:

>Start with gratitude

>Reframe setbacks as sunrise lessons

Reflection: Where do I see new light emerging?

9. The Heart in Creation — Love at the Center

Meaning: Love sustains the ecosystem of wholeness—compassion, unity, divine rhythm.

Practice:

Speak kindness to yourself and others

Do one act of care for creation

Reflection: How can I let love move through me today?

How the RISE Framework, Circle of Wholeness & Nine Pillars Work Together

Together, these three layers form an integrated ecosystem of transformation:

RISE™ — The Four Qualities of a Whole Person
Rooted · Intentional · Strong · Energized

These are the inner postures that shape how you move through the world.

The Circle of Wholeness — The Whole-Life Model

An interconnected system where physical, emotional, relational, and spiritual well-being support one another.

The Nine Pillars — The Daily Practices

Simple, repeatable habits that create sustainable change over time.

Together, they help you:

> Remember your worth
>
> Heal body, mind, and spirit
>
> Reconnect with community
>
> Establish nourishing rhythms
>
> Develop emotional stability
>
> Return to the Creator's design
>
> Transform from within

This is the foundation of your Identity & Worth journey—a return to who you were made to be.

Chapter 1 — Worth

Why Labels Can Limit Your Life

Stepping Into Your True Name

There are names we inherit before we even know language—names shaped by the tone in a room, the tension in the walls, the expression on a parent's face. Long before we learn who we are, we learn who the world believes we should be. Some labels come quietly, tucked into snide comments or family jokes. Others arrive like verdicts—sharp, permanent, spoken with the force of someone who believes they are allowed to define you.

For many of us, identity did not begin as a discovery.

It begins as a defense.

> We adapted.
>
> We performed.
>
> We learned to shrink in some places and overextend in others.
>
> We learned that being ourselves came with consequences, and being what others wanted came with praise—or at least less harm.

But identity is not fixed.

> It is not the sum of every message you absorbed.

It is not the echo of every moment someone misunderstood you.

It is not the shape you twisted yourself into just to survive.

Identity can be reclaimed.

It can be rewritten.

It can be renewed.

And worth—**your worth**—was never dependent on who labeled you. It has always existed beneath the noise, waiting for the moment that you decide to listen inward instead of outward.

This chapter is that moment.

The First Labels We Learn

I grew up learning labels the way some children learn colors—bright, sharp, and immediate. Before I understood nuance, I understood categories. My family used labels with ease, sometimes jokingly, sometimes sharply, usually without realizing the impact. But words don't have to be shouted to become heavy; the quiet ones often cut the deepest because they slip in unnoticed.

Some of the labels I received were about personality:

Too sensitive.

Too emotional.

Too quiet.

Too reactive.

Some were about roles:

The responsible one.

The strong one.

The one who doesn't complain.

Some were about pain:

The one who was hurt.

The one who "went through things."

And some were about appearance:

Bulldog nose

"Fatty, Fatty, two-by-four, can't get through the kitchen door"

Four eyes

Too big

Too different

Too much

Not enough

At the time, these labels felt like they explained me. They gave shape to what I couldn't yet articulate. But as I got older, I realized something important:

These labels didn't describe me; they described how others perceived me.

What I have learned is that often, how people perceive you has more to do with their own wounds than with your truth.

For a long time, I lived within the boundaries of those early labels that were placed on me. I stayed quiet to avoid being "too much." I carried responsibilities alone because that was "my role." I armored myself because vulnerability had, on more than one occasion, been unsafe.

What I did not yet know was that labels created to survive childhood can suffocate in adulthood.

The Labels Trauma Leaves Behind

Trauma has a way of assigning names you never asked for. Even if no one speaks them aloud, your body learns them. Fear teaches you that you are unsafe. Isolation teaches you that you are alone. Abuse teaches you that you are unworthy of tenderness. Manipulation teaches you that your reality cannot be trusted.

Trauma labels seep into identity quietly:

- Broken.
- Difficult.
- Unlovable.
- Overly emotional.
- Too much.
- Not enough.
- Dramatic.
- Damaged.

You may never say these words out loud, but you feel them in the way you hesitate to ask for help, apologize for expressing needs, or stay quiet even when something in you begs to speak.

Survival taught you habits that once protected you. But survival-mode labels do not help you build a life—they only help you avoid danger.

Healing, on the other hand, invites expansion. It invites courage. It invites truth.

But healing begins with asking:

Whose voice is this?

Who taught me this about myself?

Was any of it mine to carry?

The Labels Adulthood Reinforces

Even when we outgrow childhood and trauma-based names, adulthood has a way of assigning new ones—often sneakily.

Chronic illness can label you weak or limited.

Weight struggles can label you as undisciplined or undesirable.

Motherhood, marriage, and family roles can label you selfless, selfish, too ambitious, or not ambitious enough.

Workplaces can label you the dependable one, the quiet one, or the problem.

And in a world that thrives on comparison, it becomes frighteningly easy to let others' projections shape your self-worth.

I walked through years where my identity felt tangled in a web of external definitions—sick, struggling, too soft, too emotional, too sensitive, too opinionated, too quiet, too outspoken. I was always "too" something and "not enough" of something else.

But looking back, I realize this:

> The labels that caused me the deepest pain were the ones I accepted without questioning.

Worth erodes not from what others say—but from what we begin to believe.

Why Labels Stick

(and Why They're So Hard to Let Go)

A label becomes powerful when three things happen:

1. It is repeated.
    The brain treats repetition as truth. Even unkind truths feel familiar, and familiar feels safe—so we cling to what hurts simply because it's known.
2. It appears during vulnerability.
    Labels given during childhood, trauma, sickness, grief, or insecurity attach quickly because those moments shape self-understanding.
3. It comes from someone who holds power.
    Parents, partners, teachers, siblings, faith leaders, peers—any voice we depended on or feared leaves a more profound imprint.

Once these three converge, the label becomes a lens.

> You stop questioning it.

> You see everything through it.

> You make decisions that keep you within its boundaries.

This is how labels shape worth—not because they are true, but because they become familiar.

The Nervous System Side of Identity

This is where psychology becomes a powerful ally.

Your nervous system learns identity before your mind does.

When someone labels you negatively, your body often reacts instantly:

- Tight chest
- Stomach drop
- Shoulders curling inward
- Jaw clenching
- Throat tightening
- Heart racing
- Feeling small

These physical responses become automatic over time.

Your body remembers the label even when your mind tries to move on.

This is why changing identity feels uncomfortable.

Not because you're wrong.

Not because you're lying to yourself.

But because your nervous system is learning a new experience, and unfamiliar often feels unsafe before it feels empowering.

Healing begins with noticing your body's reaction to old labels and gently offering comfort instead of criticism.

The Slow Unraveling of Old Names

My unraveling began quietly.

Not with a bold declaration.

Not with a dramatic transformation.

Not with a sudden sense of self-worth.

It began with a whisper:

"Maybe I'm not who they said I was."

Sometimes healing starts not with confidence, but with curiosity.

I remember the early days of questioning my labels. I felt guilty for even considering that I wasn't the problem. Years of conditioning had taught me that questioning a label meant rebelling, or dishonoring someone, or risking conflict.

But the more I looked inward, the more I discovered some surprising things:

> There were parts of me that had never fit the labels others assigned.

> There were strengths hidden beneath what had once been called weaknesses.

> There were truths I had never been allowed to name.

> There was a self—quiet, persistent, and brave—waiting beneath the rubble.

Slowly, gently, I began allowing myself to imagine a truer version of me.

Identity Doesn't Begin With "I Am."

It Begins With "I Notice."

Before you can choose a new identity, you must become aware of the unconscious one you've been living.

This isn't a journal exercise, and it isn't a list; it's a lived process:

- You notice when old labels show up in your decisions.
- You notice the voice inside that calls you names others once used.
- You notice the way you shrink or overperform to match a story you didn't choose.
- You notice the tension in your body when a label feels too tight.
- You notice the shame that surfaces even when you haven't done anything wrong.

Noticing is the doorway.

Naming is the light coming in.

Choosing something new is the moment you step through.

The Gentle Power of Reclaiming Your Name

Here's something healing taught me:

> You don't erase old labels by fighting them.

> You loosen them by outgrowing them.

> Identity is fluid, adaptive, unfolding.

> You can feel strong in one season and tender in another.

> You can feel self-assured some days and questioning the next.

> You can evolve without abandoning who you used to be.

> Your past self wasn't wrong.

> You were surviving.

> You were adapting.

> You were trying to navigate a world that didn't always know how to hold you well.

Reclaiming your identity is not a rejection of your past—it is a continuation of your becoming.

When Your Story Helps Others Step Out of Hiding

One thing I've learned in the RISE Momentum Circle is this:

> When one person tells the truth, everyone breathes deeper.

When I share something vulnerable—not as a performance, not as a confession, but as an offering—it creates a doorway for others to walk through. Every week, I see it happen: someone shares a story about feeling labeled or misunderstood, and suddenly, everyone else realizes they're not alone. The room softens. Shoulders drop. People speak from deeper places.

That's the power of naming your experience with honesty:

> Your courage becomes a mirror for someone else's healing.

This book follows that same rhythm. I open the door first. I share my story not to center myself, but to create space—for you, for your truth, and for the identity you are growing into.

Worth Is Inherent, Not Assigned

Here's what I know with certainty:

Labels do not create worth.

Worth is revealed when labels fall away.

Some people find this truth spiritually grounded: the sense that a Creator establishes worth before a single opinion is formed. Others experience this truth psychologically: the understanding that worth is intrinsic to being human. And still others feel it intuitively, through quiet moments of reflection when something deeper within whispers, "I matter."

No matter how you arrive at it, the truth stands:

You are not valuable because of what someone called you.

You are valuable because you exist.

Identity grows from that truth—not from the wounds you endured, not from the stories others told about you, and not from the versions of yourself you had to become to survive.

This Is Your Beginning

You are stepping into a new chapter—not only in this book, but in your life. This is the moment you begin to look at your names with curiosity instead of fear. The moment you gently set aside the ones that harmed you. The moment you imagine who you might be without the weight of old labels.

Identity work is not quick, but it is transformative.

Worth work is not simple, but it is liberating.

Healing is not linear, but it is possible.

Your true name—the one rooted in clarity, dignity, strength, tenderness, and autonomy—has been waiting beneath all the noise.

It's time to hear it.

It's time to remember it.

It's time to become it.

And in the pages ahead, you will.

Journal Prompt

"Who Was I Before the Labels?"

Reflect on the person you were before anyone defined you.

Write about the earliest version of yourself you can remember—the child who felt, noticed, dreamed, or wondered without worrying about being "too much" or "not enough." What qualities, desires, or strengths did you naturally carry before the world began naming you?

Write down one label you've carried that no longer feels true. Beside it, write a sentence about what your own voice says instead—your voice today, not the echo of someone else's opinion.

End with this affirmation:

"I honor the truth of who I am becoming.

I am allowed to grow beyond every label that ever limited me."

Chapter 2 — Comparison: The Thief of Contentment

Remembering the Path That's Mine to Walk

Some thieves creep into identity quietly, without warning, without sound, and without the force of something obviously harmful. Comparison is one of them. It doesn't break down the door or announce its arrival. It slips into the mind like a shadow, soft at first, harmless-looking, almost reasonable. It starts as observation: Look at her progress. Look at their life. Look at what he accomplished.

But observation becomes measurement.

And measurement becomes judgment.

And judgment becomes insecurity.

Comparison is rarely loud. It whispers. It nudges. It questions. It creates an ache that feels familiar yet hard to name. And if labels shape how we see ourselves, comparison shapes how we value ourselves. Where labels confine identity, comparison starves it.

Comparison is the quiet thief that steals contentment long before we realize anything is missing.

This chapter is about reclaiming what comparison has taken—and remembering that worth is not built through measuring up to what others are doing, but through becoming who you were designed to be.

The First Time Comparison Spoke My Name

I don't remember the exact moment comparison entered my life, but I remember the sensation. It felt like a subtle tightening in my chest, a sudden awareness of being behind, a quiet belief that there must be a better version of me somewhere out there—one that looked more like someone else.

For many of us, comparison begins in childhood, long before we know its name.

>We notice the sibling who receives more praise.

>The classmate who seems to be liked effortlessly.

>The cousin who is "smarter," "prettier," "athletic," and "talented."

The subtle praise of another child becomes the silent critique of us.

And just as labels do, comparison forms grooves in the nervous system.

It becomes a reflex.

>A habit.

>A lens.

We learn early that being ourselves is not enough; we must be better, but "better" is always defined by someone else's ability, someone else's path, someone else's success.

No one sits us down and says, "Measure your life against others, child."

They don't have to.

The world teaches it effortlessly.

Every grade, every compliment, every correction, every moment of praise or disappointment becomes another brick in the measurement system we begin to live by. And by the time we're adults, comparison feels so normal we hardly notice it happening.

But what I've learned is this:

>Comparison *is not* a measurement of progress.

>Comparison *is* a measurement of insecurity.

When I first started my healing journey—the deep, internal, messy undoing—I immediately found myself comparing it to other people's healing online. They seemed so far. So whole. So steady. So enlightened. They had routines, rituals, breakthroughs, and communities. They spoke with a clarity I didn't feel yet. They shared wins I wasn't ready to claim.

And I remember thinking:

Why am I not there yet? Why is healing easier for them? What am I doing wrong?

It took me a long time to realize I wasn't behind.

I was simply measuring myself with someone else's ruler.

Comparison Is Not Harmless — It Creates a False Self

Comparison isn't just an emotional burden; it's an identity distortion.

When you compare yourself to someone else, you are no longer looking inward for truth. You're looking outward for permission. Comparison teaches you to ask questions like:

>Who should I be like?

>How do I measure up?

>What am I missing?

>What do they have that I don't?

But none of those questions leads you toward authenticity.

They lead you toward imitation.

>Comparison shifts identity outward.

>Authenticity brings identity inward.

When we compare ourselves, we begin to form a "should-be" version of ourselves—someone who looks suspiciously like everyone else but nothing like the person we were designed to become.

Here's the deeper truth:

Comparison turns identity into performance.

I spent years adapting who I was to match what I thought others expected. I softened parts of myself to avoid criticism. I intensified others to earn approval. I hid insecurities so I wouldn't seem needy. I pushed myself even harder when others seemed ahead of me. I mirrored what I saw instead of honoring who I actually was.

And slowly, comparison created a version of me that was polished on the outside but suffocating on the inside.

Comparison doesn't just steal contentment—

> It steals clarity.
>
> It steals calling.
>
> It steals courage.
>
> It steals joy.

Comparison blinds you to what you actually carry.

When I compare myself to others, I forget that God placed unique gifts, unique timing, and unique fingerprints inside me. I forget the tender way my story has been shaped. I forget that my life is not a competition—it is a calling.

Comparison convinces you that your worth is dependent on where you stand in relation to others.

Identity reminds you that your worth is dependent on nothing but truth.

How Comparison Warps the Nervous System

Comparison isn't just emotional—it's physiological.

The moment you feel "behind," your nervous system triggers a subtle survival response:

Your heart races.

Your stomach sinks.

Your mind speeds up.

Your shoulders tense.

Why?

Because comparison signals threat. Not an external threat—but an internal one: the danger of inadequacy; the warning of not belonging; the hazards of losing acceptance. The fear of not being enough.

Your nervous system doesn't know the difference between emotional danger and physical danger. It responds the same. Which means comparison doesn't just distort your identity; it destabilizes your sense of safety.

This is why comparison feels so consuming.

It's not just a thought—it's a bodily experience.

And healing comparison requires retraining the body to feel safe being exactly where you are, without rushing, without proving, without living in urgency.

Contentment is a state of the nervous system, not just a mindset.

Gratitude: The Medicine That Softens Comparison

Comparison grows in the soil of scarcity.

Gratitude grows in the soil of abundance.

You cannot hold comparison and gratitude in the same hand. They cannot coexist. One will always silence the other.

When I find myself comparing, I've learned to pause—not to shame or criticize myself, but to shift my focus. I name three things I'm deeply grateful for in that moment.

Not vague gratitude.

Not forced positivity.

But real, grounded, lived gratitude.

Gratitude doesn't magically erase the ache of comparison, but it does something far more powerful:

It recenters you.

It shifts the lens from "not enough" to "already provided."

It anchors you back into your own life.

Gratitude reminds you:

My story is unfolding.

My timing matters.

My gifts are real.

My journey is sacred.

And here's the miracle:

When you bless others rather than compare yourself to them, your heart softens.

Your defenses lower.

Your identity breathes again.

Gratitude transforms comparison into compassion—both for yourself and others.

The Lie of Being Behind — And the Truth That Replaces It

The deepest wound comparison carries is the belief that you are behind.

Behind in healing.

Behind in progress.

Behind in purpose.

Behind in becoming.

But "behind" is an illusion.

It is a lie built on the idea that there is a single timeline for everyone—a single pace, a single progression, a single path.

There is no universal timeline.

There is only yours.

Your story is not late.

Your healing is not delayed.

Your becoming is not slow.

Your journey is layered, not lagging.

If you grew up surviving more than thriving, of course, your timeline looks different. If your body carries trauma, of course, your healing takes longer. If labels shaped your identity, of course, reclaiming yourself feels slower.

But God does not rush growth.

God nurtures it.

Scripture doesn't describe humans as factories—it describes us as trees.

Rooted.

Growing.

Seasonal.

Unfolding.

No tree compares its branches to another.

It simply grows toward the light.

The truth that replaces the lie of "behind" is simple: You are right where you need to be for the lesson this moment holds.

Your timeline is handcrafted.

Your pace is purposeful.

Your unfolding is holy.

Celebrating Your Own Path — Contentment as Courage

Contentment is not stagnation.

Contentment is not apathy.

Contentment is not settling.

Contentment is confidence in your process.

Contentment is peace with your pace.

Contentment is the trust that your life is unfolding with intention.

Contentment is courage.

It takes courage to bless your path when others seem further ahead. It takes courage to honor your pace when culture tells you to hurry. It takes courage to trust your unfolding, even when you can't yet see the whole picture.

The more I've leaned into my own journey, the more I've measured progress by peace instead of performance, and the more content I've become.

I no longer need to compare my becoming to someone else's becoming. I no longer need to mirror someone else's healing. I no longer need to force a timeline that isn't mine. Contentment grows the moment you recognize God's fingerprints in your own story. And when you do, comparison loses its power.

When You Stop Comparing, You Start Becoming

Comparison keeps you stuck.

Contentment sets you free.

When you stop comparing:

> Your identity returns.

> Your joy deepens.

> Your purpose is clarified.

> Your nervous system exhales.

> Your heart remembers who it is.

The world becomes less about competition and more about calling.

Less about measurement and more about meaning.

Less about proving and more about presence.

When you stop comparing, you finally have the space to grow.

Journal Prompt

"What makes my journey uniquely mine?"

Write down:

• Three areas where you've been tempted to compare

• Three truths that remind you of your own pace, purpose, and identity

Then revisit this affirmation:

> "I release comparison and embrace contentment.

> My timeline, my gifts, and my growth are enough."

Chapter 3 — Voices: Whose Words Shape Your Worth?

Remembering Who Has Been

Speaking Into Your Story

Some influences slip into identity not by force, but by familiarity.

They don't storm the gates or announce themselves; they just settle into the background of our inner world until their sound becomes the only one we live by.

Voices are like that.

> They echo.

> They linger.

> They imprint.

A word spoken once can replay for decades.

A tone repeated often can become a script.

A belief whispered early can mold an entire identity.

Some voices lift us.

Some silence us.

Some shape us without our consent.

And some—if left unexamined—become so loud we begin to confuse them with truth.

This chapter is about recognizing the voices that have formed your worth, sifting through which ones belong, and reclaiming the authority to choose who gets to speak into your identity.

Because not every voice deserves access to the deepest parts of who you are becoming.

The First Voice That Named My Worth

I cannot pinpoint the exact moment I became aware of the voices shaping me, but I remember the way a single comment could warm me or wither me; the way silence from someone I needed could widen into an internal ache; the way certain tones felt like truth simply because I heard them often enough.

Most of us first learned our worth through the voices closest to us.

Parents. Teachers. Siblings. Peers.

Some were gentle. Some were harsh. Some were inconsistent. Some meant well, while others were meant to inflict hurt.

We remember the parent whose approval felt scarce. The teacher whose words cut sharper than they knew. The friend whose opinions felt like commandments. The bully whose insults got inside before we learned how to keep anything out. And without realizing it, those early voices began writing the script for how we saw ourselves.

They became the background music of our internal world.

Repeated often enough, they began sounding like our own thoughts.

By adulthood, many of us are carrying a collage of voices—some empowering, some oppressive, some outdated, and some not even ours to have anymore.

For years, the loudest voice in my mind sounded like perfectionism. It had the timbre of old expectations and the vocabulary of pressure. It spoke in urgencies, in warnings, in impossible standards.

It said things like, "Do more. Be better. Don't mess this up."

I didn't realize how much power that voice had until I started my healing. Only then did I understand something life-changing: The voice I had been obeying for years was not my voice at all, and it wasn't God's voice either.

The Voices That Distort Identity—Culture, Media, and the Noise of "Not Enough"

We don't just absorb voices from childhood; we absorb them from culture, too. The world speaks loudly. It speaks constantly, and it speaks with an authority it never earned.

> Be thinner.
>
> Be prettier.
>
> Be happier.
>
> Be richer.
>
> Be faster.
>
> Be visible.
>
> Be impressive.

The world speaks in comparisons, illusions, and impossible standards. It offers a sense of belonging but only on the condition of performance. It provides value based on visibility. It offers worth that can be gained today and lost tomorrow. And social media magnifies this noise.

Every scroll becomes a silent conversation: Am I doing enough? Am I achieving enough? Am I enough?

We internalize the curated lives of strangers and acquaintances as benchmarks. We measure our reality against someone else's presentation. We confuse metrics with meaning.

There was a season when scrolling became a ritual for me—one that left me more anxious than inspired, more insecure than connected. Even though I had almost a thousand "friends" on social media, people I knew or once knew, I felt more and more alone and isolated.

I didn't realize how much those images, captions, and highlight reels were shaping my worth until I noticed how I felt afterward: depleted, pressured, behind.

Eventually, I learned to step back.

Not because social media is evil, but because my soul needed space to hear something truer. Culture has a loud voice, but volume doesn't equal truth. And not every voice that speaks to you is worthy of shaping you.

The Voice That Was Always Meant to Be Loudest

God's voice does not shout over the world. It doesn't demand attention. It doesn't compete with the noise. It waits for us to quiet the noise long enough to recognize it.

His voice carries peace, not panic. Conviction, not condemnation. Direction, not confusion. Identity, not insecurity. His voice reminds you that worth is inherited, not earned. That belovedness is your beginning, not your reward, that you were formed with intention, not by some random accident.

When I read the words, "You are fearfully and wonderfully made," something inside me realigns (Psalm 139:14).

> My breath slows.

> My shoulders drop.

> The internal critic loses oxygen.

God's voice feels like coming home to myself. It names me with gentleness. It redirects me toward the truth. It never shames. It never belittles. It never speaks in the language of fear.

Learning to hear His voice wasn't about straining harder—it was about tuning in.

About becoming familiar with the tone of love so I could recognize when other voices were speaking anything less.

How Unfiltered Voices Create Inner Confusion

When too many voices speak at once—internal, external, cultural, historical—identity becomes blurry. We lose track of which thoughts are inherited and which are authentic. We confuse bias with belief. We confuse trauma with truth. We confuse criticism with calling.

Unfiltered voices create identity distortion. Before long, we adapt ourselves to survive the noise. We soften our edges to avoid criticism. We exaggerate strengths to earn approval. We hide wounds to appear strong. We diminish gifts to avoid standing out. We adopt standards that were never ours. And all the while, identity grows quieter while imitation grows louder.

One day, I paused long enough to ask a simple question:

"Is this voice truth…or fear?"

That question changed everything. It was like someone turned up the brightness in my mind. The loudest voices are rarely the truest ones. Discernment is not about silencing every voice.

It's about becoming wise enough to know which ones align with truth and which ones need to be gently escorted out of your inner world.

Strengthening Your Connection to Truth—Learning to Hear the Voice That Heals

Connection to God's voice is built slowly, relationally, intentionally. It's cultivated in rhythms of stillness, in moments of surrender, in quiet mornings where the soul can breathe again.

Hearing Him becomes easier when life is no longer filled with competing noise. His truth rises when everything else settles. His tone becomes familiar through Scripture, prayer, journaling, and in a community rooted in grace.

My morning quiet time has become my anchor. Before the world tells me who I should be, I let God remind me who I already am. Before anyone else names me, I let the One who formed me speak first. The more I listen to Him, the less power other voices carry.

His voice doesn't just guide—it protects.

It filters.

It steadies.

It restores.

And slowly, identity becomes shaped not by noise, but by clarity. Not by expectation, but by truth. Not by pressure, but by peace.

Journal Prompt

"Which voices am I allowing to define me?"

In your journal, create two columns:

- External Voices: the loudest messages influencing you today
- Truth Statements: what God says instead

Then reflect with this affirmation:

"I choose to quiet every false voice and listen for the One who calls me beloved."

Chapter 4 — Shame vs. Conviction: Learning the Difference

Some burdens feel heavy, *not* because they are true, but because they have been carried for too long.

Shame is like that.

It settles into the body quietly, disguising itself as responsibility, humility, or self-awareness. It pretends to be helpful. It masquerades as motivation. But over time, it begins to weigh down identity instead of shaping character. It doesn't correct behavior—it erodes worth. It doesn't point forward—it presses downward. And if left unnamed, shame becomes one of the most powerful identity-shaping forces in a person's life.

Conviction, on the other hand, feels different. Even when it's uncomfortable, it carries a strange clarity. It does not confuse who you are with what you did. It does not strip dignity in order to demand change. Conviction speaks to alignment. Shame, on the other hand, speaks to annihilation.

This chapter is about learning to tell the difference.

Because when shame and conviction get tangled together, healing stalls. Growth becomes punishment. Repentance becomes self-hatred. And identity becomes something to be earned back instead of something to be restored.

The Weight of Shame and the Way It Rewrites Identity

Shame does not simply say, "Something went wrong."

Shame says, "Something is wrong with you."

That distinction matters more than we realize.

Most people can name moments when they felt shame—but fewer can trace how shame quietly shaped the way they saw themselves afterward. Shame doesn't always arrive dramatically. Sometimes it comes through in a casual sentence. A look of disappointment. A rule applied without compassion. A belief absorbed before language was fully formed.

Shame lodges itself in memory and muscle. It tightens the chest. It shortens the breath. It pulls the eyes downward. It creates a reflexive desire to hide—not just from others, but from oneself.

For many of us, shame became the lens through which we learned to interpret mistakes, trauma, and unmet expectations. We learned early that certain experiences made us "less than," even when we had no language to challenge that belief. Shame taught us to examine ourselves for fault even in situations where fault never belonged to us.

I remember the first time shame attached itself to my identity clearly—not because it was dramatic, but because it was devastatingly quiet. A statement was made, rooted in generational prejudice and unexamined belief: "Any woman who gets raped was asking for it."

At twelve years old, I did not have the tools to interrogate that statement. I only had a developing sense of self and a deep desire to be safe and loved. So, I turned inward. I examined myself relentlessly. I searched for what I must have done wrong. What I must have been. What signal must I have given?

That is what shame does—it forces the wounded to become the investigator of their own pain.

Years later, I would understand the cultural and generational roots of that belief. I would recognize the projection, the misinformation, the inheritance of blame that had nothing to do with me. I would understand that the statement was a lie, and that there was nothing I did to provoke the abuse, and there was nothing I could have done to prevent it. The responsibility was not mine.

But shame does not dissolve simply because logic arrives. Shame embeds itself emotionally before truth ever has a chance to speak.

And once shame attaches to identity, it becomes a lens—not an event.

Why Shame Thrives in Silence

Shame needs secrecy to survive.

It feeds on isolation. It grows in the absence of compassionate witnesses. It convinces us that exposure will destroy us rather than free us. Shame whispers that if others really knew, love would disappear.

That whisper is powerful.

So, we learn to compartmentalize. We present curated versions of ourselves. We become adept at appearing functional while quietly believing we are fundamentally flawed. Shame teaches us to perform worthiness rather than inhabit it.

And perhaps most dangerously, shame mimics responsibility. It convinces us that self-punishment is the same thing as accountability. That self-loathing is humility. That carrying the weight forever is proof of sincerity.

But shame never produces transformation—it produces paralysis.

It keeps us stuck reliving moments rather than learning from them. It turns growth into penance. It teaches us to expect rejection even in spaces meant for healing.

Conviction does none of this.

What Healthy Conviction Actually Feels Like

Conviction has been misunderstood, especially in religious contexts. Too often, it has been weaponized—used to control behavior, enforce conformity, or shame people into compliance. But true conviction is not coercive. It is not loud. It does not humiliate.

Healthy conviction feels like a nudge, not a hammer.

It arises from alignment with values—from the quiet recognition that something does not reflect who you are becoming. It does not collapse identity into behavior. Instead, it appeals to identity as the reason change is possible.

Conviction sounds like, "This isn't who you want to be."

Shame sounds like, "This is who you are."

Conviction invites you back into integrity; whereas shame pushes you out of a relationship with yourself, with others, and with God.

When conviction is healthy, it carries hope. It assumes restoration is possible. It believes growth is within reach. It motivates without crushing. It corrects without condemning.

For me, conviction has never felt like fear. It has felt like remembering. Like an internal compass recalibrating. Like a quiet reminder that I am capable of better—not because I am deficient, but because I am loved.

Conviction motivates me. Shame immobilized me.

That difference changed everything.

Shame's Greatest Lie: Identity Reduction

One of shame's most destructive tactics is identity reduction.

It takes a moment, a failure, a wound, or a struggle and turns it into a definition. It collapses complexity into condemnation. It rewrites language so that behavior becomes belief.

"I failed" becomes "I am a failure."

"I was hurt" becomes "I am broken."

"I made a mistake" becomes "I am a mistake."

Once identity is reduced, hope narrows. Possibility shrinks. The future feels predetermined by the past. And healing feels inaccessible—not because it is impossible, but because shame convinces us we don't deserve it.

Shame told me for years that I was beyond repair. That something fundamental had been damaged beyond restoration. That love would always be conditional. That safety would always be temporary.

But shame was lying.

Truth revealed something radically different: restoration is not a reward—it is a birthright. Worth is not fragile—it is inherent. Healing is not permission-based—it is offered freely.

What once felt like ruin became soil. What once felt like evidence against me became ground for renewal. Shame did not get the final word.

Grace as the Antidote to Shame

Grace does not deny responsibility—but it reframes it.

Grace says that worth does not fluctuate based on performance. That failure does not revoke belonging. That learning does not require humiliation. Grace allows us to see ourselves as humans in process rather than problems to be fixed.

For a long time, my response to falling short was harshness. Internal lectures. Endless replay. Emotional punishment. I believed that if I were hard enough on myself, I would change faster.

I was wrong.

Change came when grace entered the conversation.

Grace invited curiosity instead of condemnation. Reflection instead of rumination. Growth instead of guilt spirals. Grace did not excuse behavior, but it removed the need for self-destruction as proof of remorse.

Grace softened the internal environment enough for truth to take root.

When grace became part of my healing, responsibility became empowering instead of crushing. Mistakes became information instead of identity statements. And repentance became relational instead of punitive.

Grace did not lower the standard—it made it sustainable.

Moving from Shame to Freedom

Freedom does not begin with forgetting the past. It begins with naming what has been carried.

Shame loses power when it is exposed to compassion. When compassionate words are spoken aloud. When grace is written down. When shame is met with truth instead of secrecy. Healing begins when we stop protecting shame and start protecting truth.

Freedom also requires replacing false narratives. Shame stories must be rewritten—not through denial, but through alignment with what is real.

When shame says, "You'll never change," truth responds, "You already are."

When shame says, "You are defined by your worst moment," truth responds, "You are defined by love."

When shame says, "Hide," truth says, "Come home."

Freedom is not pretending perfection. It is walking honestly. It is choosing truth again and again, even when shame resurfaces. Because healing is not linear—but it is possible.

And conviction—true conviction—will always point toward freedom, never away from it.

Learning to Discern the Voices

If shame and conviction sound similar to you, that does not mean you are broken—it means you were taught incorrectly.

Discernment is learned. Tone matters. Fruit matters. Outcome matters.

Shame leaves you smaller, quieter, and afraid.

Conviction leaves you clearer, grounded, and hopeful.

One isolates. The other reconnects.

One attacks identity. The other protects it.

Learning the difference is not just theological—it is psychological. It is emotional. It is embodied. And it is essential for healing.

Journal Prompt

"What's the difference between guilt that guides and shame that condemns?"

Reflect on a recent moment where both appeared.

What was the message of shame?

What would conviction say instead?

Rewrite the shame message into a truth statement grounded in grace.

Then close with this affirmation:

"Shame no longer defines me. I welcome conviction that leads to change and grace that restores my worth."

Because healing does not require self-destruction.

It requires truth, compassion, and the courage to choose a different voice.

And that voice—when it is truly aligned—will always lead you home.

Chapter 5 — The Stories We Tell Ourselves: Rewriting Internal Narratives

Some stories don't live on paper.

They live in the nervous system.

> In the way we brace before a conversation.

> In the way we apologize for taking up space.

> In the way we assume rejection before anyone has even spoken.

We don't just live life. We interpret it. And that interpretation becomes a story.

> A story about who we are.

> A story about what we can expect from people.

> A story about what we are allowed to want.

> A story about what we deserve.

And most of the time, we don't even realize we're telling it, because many of our deepest internal narratives were written early—when we were too young to fact-check the message, too vulnerable to challenge the tone, and too dependent to risk questioning the people who shaped our world. Some stories were formed by words that were spoken. Others were formed through what was never said. Through silence. Through absence. Through inconsistency. Through being praised only when we performed, and overlooked when we were simply human.

Over time, those experiences became meaningful. And the meaning that gets assigned to those experiences shapes identity.

This chapter is about noticing the story you've been living under—especially the parts you did not consciously choose—and beginning the sacred work of rewriting.

Not by pretending the past did not happen.

Not by forcing positivity over pain.

But by bringing truth to the places where fear used to be the narrator.

The Story Beneath the Story

Most people can tell you the facts of their lives, but fewer can name the story those facts taught them to believe.

The facts might be: My parents divorced.

The story might be: People leave.

The facts might be: I was criticized often.

The story might be: I'm never quite enough.

The facts might be: I was abused, violated, or betrayed.

The story might be: My body isn't safe. I'm dirty. I'm to blame.

The facts might be: I had to grow up fast.

The story might be: I can't need anything. I have to handle it alone.

These are not just thoughts. They become frameworks. They become internal laws we live by. They shape who we trust, what we tolerate, how we love, how we work, and how we speak to ourselves in the quiet moments when no one is watching.

And because these stories were often written during pain, they can feel permanent. Like the world has already decided who we are.

But pain is not a prophet.

Just because a story was formed in survival does not mean it has the authority to shape your future.

"I Have to Earn Love" and Other Hidden Scripts

For years, my internal story was simple, even if I never said it out loud:

I have to earn love.

It showed up in how I overworked.

How I overgave.

How I over-explained.

How I over-apologized.

I acted as if love was a wage I had to deserve, not a gift I was allowed to receive. I moved through relationships as if my belonging could be revoked at any moment, so I stayed useful. I stayed agreeable. I stayed "good."

And that story shaped my entire nervous system.

Because when you believe love must be earned, you are never fully at rest. You are always scanning for disapproval. You are always measuring your performance. You are always afraid that one mistake will cost you a connection.

That story did not come from truth.

It came from fear.

And fear is an eager author—it writes quickly and edits harshly.

But the moment I recognized that script for what it was, something changed. Not instantly. Not magically. But noticeably. Because awareness weakens old stories, it interrupts the automatic replay.

I began to see the pattern: when I felt unsafe, I performed. When I felt unsure, I over-functioned. When I feared rejection, I tried to become indispensable.

And then I began writing a new line, slowly, one sentence at a time:

> Love is not something I earn. Love is something I receive.

How Thoughts Become Beliefs—and Beliefs Become Identity

Thoughts are not harmless. Especially repeated ones.

> A thought you think once is a visitor.

> A thought you think every day becomes a resident.

Repeated thoughts carve pathways in the brain. They become familiar routes, well-worn roads the mind defaults to, especially when stressed. The brain loves efficiency. It will choose a familiar story even if it is painful, simply because it is known.

That is how a thought becomes a belief.

> And a belief becomes a lens.

> And a lens becomes identity.

This is why the stories we tell ourselves matter so much.

If you repeatedly think, I'm too much, you begin shrinking.

If you repeatedly think, I'm a burden, you stop asking for help.

If you repeatedly think, I'll never change, you stop trying.

If you repeatedly think, People can't be trusted, you stop letting anyone close.

And then one day, you look up and realize your life has been shaped by a script you never chose.

I used to think: I'll never change.

It felt like a conclusion. Like a verdict. Like a final sentence.

But healing taught me something that disrupted that belief: a thought is not truth. A thought is often a reflection of experience, fear, conditioning, or trauma. It can be loud. It can be persuasive. It can feel familiar. But it is not automatically reliable.

The moment I recognized that "I'll never change" was a loop—not a prophecy—it lost power. Not all power. But enough power for me to begin speaking differently.

> I'm learning.
>
> I'm growing.
>
> I'm being renewed.
>
> I'm not finished.

New thoughts are fragile at first. They feel unfamiliar. Sometimes they feel fake. That does not mean they are wrong. It means they are new.

Lies vs. Truth in Self-Talk

One of the most important skills in healing is learning to test the voice in your head.

> Not every thought is yours.
>
> Not every thought is true.
>
> Not every thought deserves agreement.

Lies often sound urgent. They pressure. They threaten. They predict disaster. They speak in absolutes:

> Always.
>
> Never.
>
> Everyone.
>
> No one.
>
> You'll fail again.

Nothing will change.

Lies create fear, panic, hopelessness, and collapse.

Truth creates clarity, steadiness, and direction.

Truth does not always feel comfortable—but it feels clean. It does not leave residue. It does not leave you smaller. It does not shame you into silence. Truth may correct you, but it does not crush you.

For those who walk with God, this becomes even clearer over time: truth aligns with His character. It carries the tone of love, even when it challenges. It calls you higher without calling you worthless. It invites repentance without requiring self-hatred.

And for those who do not use spiritual language, the same discernment still applies: truth aligns with dignity. It aligns with your deepest values. It aligns with what is life-giving, grounded, and real.

I can often tell it's a lie by what it does to my body.

When I believe a lie, I tense.

> My chest tightens.

> My thoughts spiral.

> My nervous system shifts into urgency or despair.

When I return to truth, my breath opens.

> My shoulders drop.

> My mind clears.

Truth feels like room to move.

Lies feel like a closing hallway.

Rewriting with Truth and Grace

Rewriting an internal narrative is not a one-time declaration. It is a practice. It is a daily decision to stop letting old fear be the narrator.

And rewriting does not mean you erase the old story. The old story mattered. It formed in real moments. It protected you in real ways. Sometimes the old story was the best your younger self could do to make sense of pain.

So, the goal is not self-contempt for having that story. The goal is compassion—and new authorship.

Rewriting usually happens in three movements:

Awareness: What is the story I keep telling?

Compassion: Why did I start believing this? What was I trying to survive?

Practice: What truth will I choose now, and how will I reinforce it?

Journaling helps because when a story is vague, it feels like reality. But when you write it down, you can finally see it as language—something that can be edited.

Scripture helps those who draw life from it because it gives you a voice outside of your fear. It reminds you what love actually sounds like.

Therapy helps because some stories were formed in deep relational harm and need a safe witness to unwind.

Community helps because shame-based narratives dissolve faster in the presence of compassionate people.

And grace helps because it changes the tone of the rewrite.

Without grace, rewriting becomes another performance: "I must think perfectly." With grace, rewriting becomes healing: "I can practice truth gently."

I rewrote my old story of "I'm damaged" into "I'm being restored." And every time I say it, it feels like healing ink rewriting my pages.

Not because the past vanishes—but because the meaning changes.

What Your Redeemed Story Sounds Like Now

Healing does not erase your past. It redeems it.

It means the hardest chapters are no longer the conclusion.

It means your story is no longer about what happened to you.

It becomes about what happened **in** you.

There is a difference between a trauma story and a redeemed story.

A trauma story says: "This is what was done to me, and it proves who I am."

A redeemed story says: "This is what happened, and it did not get the final word."

A trauma story ends in survival.

A redeemed story continues into transformation.

And that does not mean everything is fixed. Redemption is not denial. It is not pretending. It is not spiritualizing pain away. Redemption is when truth becomes louder than the wound.

My story used to be about survival. Now it is about restoration. I'm still being written. But this time, I know who the Author really is.

Journal Prompt:

"What story am I ready to rewrite?"

Write one paragraph of your old narrative and one paragraph of your new truth.

End with this affirmation:

"I am not my past story. I am being rewritten in truth, grace, and purpose."

Chapter 6 — Resilience: Bouncing Back Without Losing Yourself

Resilience is often misunderstood.

It gets portrayed as toughness. As grit. As pushing through without complaint. As standing strong no matter the cost. But that version of resilience leaves you exhausted, disconnected, and quietly brittle inside.

True resilience is not about refusing to break.

It is about bending without losing your roots.

It is the ability to be changed by hardship without being erased by it.

> To feel deeply without collapsing.
>
> To adapt without abandoning yourself.
>
> To move forward without pretending that nothing hurts.

Most of us learned resilience in survival mode. We learned how to keep going because stopping felt dangerous. We learned how to function because falling apart did not feel like an option. And in those seasons, resilience looked like endurance, not wholeness.

But endurance alone is not the same as resilience.

Resilience is what allows you to remain yourself even when life rearranges everything around you.

This chapter is about reclaiming resilience as something humane, rooted, and identity-preserving—not something that hardens you, numbs you, or forces you to disappear to survive.

When Life Tests Strength and Identity at the Same Time

Some challenges test your strength. Others test your identity. And the hardest seasons in life tend to test both at once. Challenges may look like:

> A loss that strips away a role you once relied on.

> A betrayal that shakes your sense of safety.

> A diagnosis that alters how you see your body.

> A season of burnout that forces you to admit your limits.

> A trauma that interrupts the story you thought your life would tell.

In those moments, resilience is not theoretical. It becomes personal.

I learned this when my life fell apart in ways I could not fix quickly or quietly. What unraveled was not just my circumstances, but my sense of self. The version of resilience I had practiced for years—keep going, stay strong, do not show weakness—no longer worked. Pretending I was fine cost me more than admitting that I wasn't.

That season taught me something I had never fully understood: resilience does not mean denying pain. It means trusting that you are still held inside the pain. That you can fall apart without falling away from who you are.

That realization changed everything. Because resilience rooted in denial eventually collapses. Resilience rooted in truth deepens.

Healthy Resilience vs. Emotional Numbing

One of the most important distinctions to make in healing is the difference between resilience and numbing.

They can look similar from the outside.

> Both can appear calm.

> Both can look functional.

> Both can keep life moving forward.

But internally, they are worlds apart.

Emotional numbing avoids. It suppresses. It disconnects. It says, "I don't have time to feel this." It bypasses grief, fear, and anger in order to stay operational. Over time, numbing dulls joy just as much as it does the pain. It protects in the short term but costs connection in the long run.

Healthy resilience feels. It allows emotion to move through the body, without letting emotion become identity. It does not rush healing, and it doesn't shame vulnerability. It honors what hurts while still choosing wisdom in how to respond.

For a long time, I mistook numbing for strength. I prided myself on not crying. On staying composed. On handling things alone. I thought resilience meant emotional silence.

> But silence is not strength.

> Presence is.

True resilience allowed me to feel sadness without drowning in it. To feel anger without becoming it. To feel fear without obeying it. I learned that emotions are signals, not verdicts. They deserve attention, yes, but they do not deserve authority.

That shift—from numbing to feeling—did not make me weaker. It made me more integrated. More alive. More of myself.

Staying Anchored When Everything Else Changes

Life changes faster than identity *if* identity is rooted in something solid. But when identity is built primarily on roles, performance, or circumstances, change can feel like annihilation. A job ends, and worth collapses. A relationship shifts, and identity feels lost. A season ends, and you no longer know who you are. Resilience without an anchor becomes exhaustion.

The deeper work is learning what remains when everything else changes.

Roles shift.

Titles come and go.

Capacity fluctuates.

Circumstances evolve.

But worth does not.

I learned this the hard way when I lost a job that had quietly become intertwined with my sense of value. Without the title, I felt unsteady. I questioned myself. I questioned my usefulness. I questioned my future.

That loss forced a reckoning: Who am I when the role disappears?

And slowly, through prayer, reflection, and rebuilding, I realized my value had never been in the title. It had been in my being. In the truth that I am known, seen, and loved beyond what I produce.

When identity is anchored in truth—whether that truth is framed spiritually, ethically, or relationally—it becomes portable. You carry it with you through transitions. You grieve losses without losing yourself. You adapt without erasing your essence.

That is resilience with roots.

Rebuilding After Setbacks Without Rushing the Process

Resilience grows in rhythm, not urgency.

After a setback, the instinct is often to bounce back quickly—to return to normal, to prove strength, to minimize disruption. But rushing recovery can create fragile resilience that fractures later.

Rebuilding requires patience. Rest is not laziness; it is repair. Reflection is not dwelling; it is integration. Renewal is not instant; it is cumulative.

After burnout, I had to learn how to rebuild slowly. Not dramatically. Not heroically. But faithfully. One walk. One journal entry. One prayer. One deep breath. One honest conversation.

Resilience is built in those small, repeated acts of self-attunement. In learning when to pause instead of pushing. In listening to the body's wisdom instead of overriding it.

The goal is not to return to who you were before. The goal is to become wiser, more grounded, and more whole than before.

Resilience does not rewind the story.

It deepens it.

When Resilience Becomes Compassion and Purpose

Pain that is processed becomes wisdom.

Pain that is integrated becomes empathy.

One of the quiet gifts of resilience is that it changes how you see others. Hardship softens the places where judgment once lived. It expands compassion. It creates space for nuance. It allows you to sit with someone else's pain without needing to fix it. What once hurt you can become a place of connection—when shared with humility, not heroism.

I used to resent my struggles. I saw them as detours, delays, and disadvantages. But over time, I began to see them differently. They taught me patience. They taught me tenderness. They taught me how to listen. They taught me how to hold space.

My resilience did not make me superior. It made me more human. And that humanity became part of my purpose—not as a badge, but as a bridge.

Your scars are not proof of failure. They are evidence of survival and growth. They remind you not of what broke you, but of what did not.

Resilience Without Losing Yourself

Resilience does not mean you become unrecognizable.

It means you become more yourself—stripped of illusions, anchored in truth, softened by compassion, and strengthened by integration.

You are resilient not because you never fall, but because you rise without abandoning your heart.

You are resilient because you bend and still remain rooted.

You are resilient because you let hardship shape you without letting it shrink you.

And you are allowed to define resilience in a way that keeps you whole.

Journal Prompt:

"What have I learned about who I am through what I've survived?"

List three experiences that tested you—and write one lesson or strength each revealed.

End with this affirmation:

"I am resilient, not because I never fall, but because I rise each time—wiser, softer, and still myself."

Chapter 7 — Authenticity: Removing the Masks

Most masks are not chosen consciously.

They are crafted quietly, over time, in moments when being ourselves did not feel safe. They form when honesty was punished, when emotions were dismissed, when vulnerability was met with judgment, or when love felt conditional. Long before we knew the word authenticity, we learned how to read a room. We learned what was welcomed and what was not. And we adapted.

We learned how to perform.

>Some masks look like strength.

>Some look like competence.

>Some look like cheerfulness.

>Some look like spiritual maturity.

>Some look like silence.

And many of them worked—at least for a while. They helped us belong. They helped us survive. They helped us avoid rejection. But what protects us early can imprison us later. Because the longer we live behind a mask, the harder it becomes to remember who we are underneath it.

This chapter is not about exposing everything or tearing down all protection at once. Authenticity is not reckless honesty. It is not oversharing. It is not turning vulnerability into a performance of its own. Authenticity is quieter than that.

Authenticity is alignment.

It is the slow, courageous practice of being honest with yourself first—and then allowing that honesty to shape how you show up in the world.

The Masks We Wear to Feel Safe

Every mask begins as a solution.

"I'm fine" mask protects you from burdening others.

The "strong one" mask protects you from being disappointed again.

The "good one" mask protects you from criticism.

The "successful one" mask protects you from feeling replaceable.

The "spiritual one" mask protects you from doubt and uncertainty.

None of these masks are evil. They are intelligent responses to environments that taught us certain parts of ourselves were risky. And for a time, they often worked. They earned praise. They avoided conflict. They kept us included.

But masks come with a cost.

The cost is internal fragmentation—the quiet sense that the version of you the world knows is not the full truth. The cost is exhaustion from maintaining an image. The cost is loneliness, even in rooms full of people. Because connection requires presence, and presence requires honesty.

For years, my most familiar mask was "I'm fine."

Even when I wasn't.

Especially when I wasn't.

That mask helped me keep moving. It kept people from asking questions I didn't know how to answer. It kept me from having to sit with pain I didn't yet have language for. But it also kept me unseen. And over time, it taught me to abandon myself before anyone else could.

Taking that mask off felt dangerous at first. Vulnerability always does when it's unfamiliar. But what surprised me was not rejection—it was relief. Honesty made room for real connection. It gave others permission to be human, too. And slowly, I learned that being real was not the same as being unsafe.

What Hiding Does to the Soul

Hiding is exhausting! Not because we are weak, but because pretending requires constant vigilance. You have to remember who you are supposed to be. You have to manage perception. You have to suppress emotion. You have to stay "on."

Over time, this creates an internal split: the public self and the private self. The version of you that performs, and the version of you that feels. The version that is acceptable, and the version that is true.

That split takes a toll.

Emotionally, hiding leads to disconnection—from others and from yourself. It dulls intuition. It blurs desire. It creates confusion about what you actually feel versus what you think you should feel.

Physically, hiding shows up in tension. Tight shoulders. Shallow breath. Chronic fatigue. A nervous system that never fully rests.

Spiritually, hiding interrupts intimacy. Whether you name God or simply truth, healing requires honesty. You cannot be restored in the places you refuse to acknowledge. Wholeness is not about perfection—it is about integration.

I didn't realize how heavy my masks were until I began setting them down. Living honestly did not make life easier—but it made it lighter. There is peace in no longer having to perform your way into belonging.

The Fear of Being Seen

At the root of most masks is fear.

> Fear of judgment.

> Fear of rejection.

> Fear of being misunderstood.

Fear of being "too much."

Fear of not being enough.

Many of us learned—explicitly or implicitly—that love had conditions. That approval could be withdrawn. That being fully known was risky. So, we edited ourselves. We learned to hide the parts that felt inconvenient, emotional, or messy.

And suddenly the fear makes perfect sense.

If being real once led to pain, the nervous system remembers. It tries to protect you by keeping vulnerability behind glass. But protection can become a prison when fear is allowed to make the rules indefinitely.

For a long time, I believed that if people truly saw my flaws, they would leave. That belief kept me polished but distant. Capable but alone. What I learned, slowly and tenderly, was that the right people do not require perfection. They require presence.

Real love cannot connect with a mask.

It connects with truth—imperfect, evolving, human truth.

Authenticity With Wisdom and Boundaries

One of the biggest misconceptions about authenticity is that it requires complete transparency in every setting. It does not.

Authenticity is not about telling everyone everything. It is about not lying—to yourself or to others—about who you are.

Boundaries are not the opposite of authenticity; they are what make authenticity sustainable. You can be real without being exposed. You can be honest without being unsafe. You can be vulnerable selectively, wisely, and with discernment.

There is a difference between transparency and vulnerability.

Transparency is information.

Vulnerability is presence.

You can share facts without sharing your heart.

And you can share your heart without sharing every detail.

Authenticity asks different questions than oversharing does:

> Is this true?
>
> Is this kind?
>
> Is this appropriate for this space?
>
> Does this honor my values and my peace?

I have learned that being authentic does not mean explaining myself to everyone. It means I stop negotiating with the truth inside myself. I stop pretending. I let my yes be yes, my no be no, and my identity be grounded rather than performative.

That is freedom with wisdom.

Living Without the Mask

Authenticity is alignment—when your inner life and outer life begin to agree.

It looks like your words matching your values.

> Your boundaries matching your needs.
>
> Your relationships matching your capacity.
>
> Your faith matching your lived compassion.

When you remove the mask, you do not become reckless. You become coherent.

Living authentically does not mean you never struggle. It means you stop hiding the struggle from yourself. It means you show up as you are—growing, learning, healing.

For me, living authentically now means I no longer shrink to make others comfortable. I no longer perform for approval. I no longer confuse being liked with being loved.

I can be seen as I am: loved, imperfect, and still becoming.

And that is more than enough.

Journal Prompt:

"Who am I when no one's watching?"

List five ways you can live more honestly—with yourself, God, and others.

End with this affirmation:

"I am free to be fully seen. I am not who I pretend to be—I am who I am becoming in truth and grace."

Chapter 8 — Identity in Transitions: When Roles Change

Transitions rarely ask permission.

They arrive quietly or all at once, expected or uninvited, gentle or disruptive. A role ends. A season shifts. A body changes. A relationship evolves. And suddenly, the identity you have been living inside no longer fits the life you are standing in.

Transitions do not just change circumstances.

They challenge the stories we have told ourselves about who we are.

When roles change, it can feel like losing a part of yourself. The job that once defined your days is gone. The children who once needed you constantly no longer do. The body you relied on asks for new limits. The relationship you built your future around is no longer there.

And in the quiet that follows, a question emerges—sometimes softly, sometimes with urgency:

If I'm not this anymore… who am I now?

This chapter is about navigating that question without panic or self-erasure. It is about learning how to let roles change without letting worth collapse. It is about discovering that identity "rooted in being" can survive transitions that "identity rooted in doing" cannot.

When Transitions Shake Identity

Roles give structure to our lives. They organize time, responsibilities, and belonging. They provide us with language for who we are in the world: parent, partner, caregiver, provider, leader, professional, helper.

There is nothing wrong with roles. They are meaningful. They matter. But when a role becomes the primary container for identity, change can feel destabilizing rather than developmental.

A transition does not just remove what you do.

It removes the mirror you were using to see yourself.

When my career ended unexpectedly, the loss felt deeper than employment. I felt invisible. Untethered. Unnamed. Without the role, I struggled to locate my value. My days were quieter, but my internal world was louder. My internal world was filled with questions, yes about how I was going to pay bills or put food on the table, but also filled with questions about relevance, purpose, and usefulness.

What surprised me most was not the grief, but the fear. Fear that without the role, I would disappear. Fear that I would no longer matter in the same way. Fear that the best version of me was behind me.

But that season became a threshold rather than a dead end.

Over time, I realized I wasn't losing myself—I was being redefined. The pause created space to notice parts of me that had been overshadowed by productivity. My value did not end with my title. It deepened when I was forced to sit with who I was beneath it.

Transitions often feel like subtraction. But many are invitations into expansion.

Why We Tie Worth to Roles

We are not born equating worth with performance. We learn it.

From an early age, approval often follows achievement. Praise follows productivity. Belonging follows contribution. Slowly, subtly, the message forms:

> What you do is who you are.

Culture reinforces this belief relentlessly. We are asked what we do before we are asked how we are. We are rewarded for output, efficiency, and visibility. Rest is seen as laziness. Slowing down feels like falling behind.

Roles become proof of value.

So, when a role changes or ends, the nervous system often responds with alarm. Confidence drops. Self-doubt rises. Shame creeps in. We may rush to fill the void with another role, another responsibility, another identity—anything to avoid the discomfort of not knowing.

For years, I defined myself as "the caretaker." I was the one others relied on. The one who held things together. The one who anticipated needs. That role gave me purpose and a sense of belonging—but it also consumed me.

When that season ended, I felt lost. I did not know how to relate to myself without the constant demand. Learning that my worth was not dependent on being needed was both terrifying and freeing.

Separating worth from role is not about rejecting responsibility.

It is about remembering that responsibility is not the source of identity.

Transitions as Sacred Opportunities

Every transition carries loss. That loss deserves to be named and honored. Even positive transitions include grief for what was familiar, predictable, and known.

But transitions also carry possibility.

They interrupt autopilot. They slow us down enough to ask better questions. They expose what was never meant to be permanent. And they invite us into a deeper relationship with truth.

In unfamiliar seasons, faith is stretched—not always in dramatic ways, but in quiet trust. Trust that identity can survive uncertainty. Trust that worth does not evaporate when the external scaffolding shifts. Trust that becoming is still happening, even when progress looks invisible.

During a health challenge, I discovered a strength I had never known. It was not the strength of pushing through or proving resilience. It was the strength of listening. Of honoring limits. Of allowing rest to be part of faithfulness.

That season taught me that strength does not always roar. Sometimes it whispers, "Slow down." Sometimes it says, "Let this change you."

Transitions are not thieves by default.

Many are teachers—if we are willing to listen.

Staying Grounded When Everything Feels Unfamiliar

When external anchors disappear, internal ones become essential.

Grounding does not require certainty. It requires consistency. Small rhythms remind the body and soul that safety does not depend on the stability of circumstances.

Rituals help. Not because they fix the transition, but because they hold you within it. A morning breath. A walk outside. Lighting a candle. Writing one honest sentence and returning to prayer, Scripture, nature, or community.

These practices are not escapes.

They are reminders.

When life felt unsteady, I returned to simplicity. I created small rituals that anchored me in the present moment. Those acts did not answer all my questions—but they reminded me that peace could coexist with uncertainty.

We cannot control change. But we can choose our posture within it.

Grounding practices help us stay connected to who we are, even when we are not yet sure who we are becoming.

Becoming Without Losing What Was

One of the greatest fears in transition is that honoring what comes next will dishonor what came before. But growth does not erase the past—it integrates it.

You are not losing your identity.

You are uncovering its deeper layers.

Every role you have held has taught you something true about yourself. Caregiving revealed compassion. Leadership revealed responsibility. Work revealed creativity. Parenting revealed endurance. Even painful roles revealed resilience and wisdom.

When a role ends, the lesson does not disappear. Becoming is not a betrayal of who you were. It is a continuation.

I used to fear change because it felt like erasure. Now I see it as refinement. Each season strips away what is temporary so that what is lasting can surface. Less defined by function. More characterized by essence.

I am still becoming.

But now I am less afraid of the process.

Journal Prompt:

"Who am I becoming in this season of change?"

Reflect on three past transitions and write one truth you gained from each.

End with this affirmation:

"My identity is not lost in transition—it is strengthened through transformation. I am grounded, growing, and guided through every change."

Chapter 9 — Faith & Worth: Rooting Identity in Being Inherently Beloved

There is a particular kind of exhaustion that comes from trying to prove you deserve to exist.

It does not always announce itself as striving. Sometimes it looks like being responsible. Being helpful. Being "good." Being high-achieving. Being reliable. Being needed. But underneath those behaviors is often the same trembling question:

> Am I still worthy if I stop performing?
>
> Am I still lovable if I disappoint someone?
>
> Am I still valuable if I rest?

Many of us were taught—directly or subtly—that worth has conditions. That approval must be earned. That love must be maintained. That belonging is something we can lose if we do not keep up.

So, we hustle for safety.

We shape-shift to be accepted. We become what people praise. We hide what people punish. We learn the art of staying impressive, even if it costs us peace. And over time, the nervous system begins to treat worth like a fragile object—something that can shatter with one mistake.

But inherent worth is not fragile.

It is not built on performance. It is not sustained by productivity. It does not evaporate when you struggle or fluctuate when your emotions dip. It does not depend on whether you are currently "winning" in life. Inherent worth is what remains when everything else is stripped away.

This chapter is about returning to that truth, about rooting identity in being inherently beloved—whether you understand "beloved" through faith in God, spiritual trust, inner values, human dignity, or a guiding sense of meaning larger than the self. Because the world will always offer you a counterfeit form of worth:

worth that rises and falls with output, appearance, approval, and success.

But there is another kind of worth.

> Worth that is inherited, not achieved.

> Worth that is secure, not negotiated.

> Worth that anchors you when life tries to measure you.

What It Means to Be Beloved

The word beloved can feel tender or threatening depending on your history.

For some, it lands like warmth—like a blanket, like belonging, like being chosen without having to perform. For others, it triggers skepticism. Because if love was conditional growing up, the idea of being beloved for simply existing can feel impossible, like a concept meant for someone else.

But belovedness is not a mood. It is not a reward. It is not a title given only to the worthy.

Beloved means your value is intact.

> Even when your emotions are messy.

> Even when your life is uncertain.

> Even when your productivity is low.

> Even when you are grieving.

Even when you are healing.

Even when you are resting.

To be beloved is to be valuable without auditioning.

And that truth is disruptive, because it removes the currency many of us have been using to buy a sense of worth. If your worth is inherent, then you do not have to spend your life proving you deserve to be here.

For a long time, I believed I had to prove my worth through achievement—through being competent, composed, useful, and "good enough." Even my healing felt like something I had to accomplish correctly. I thought if I could just become the best version of myself, then I would finally be safe to love.

But when I began to understand that my worth was not something I had to earn, something deep inside my core softened.

I stopped striving as my default posture.

I started allowing myself to breathe.

I started letting rest be part of being human.

Belovedness did not make me passive. It made me grounded. When worth becomes secure, life becomes less frantic.

Faith, Trust, and a Grounding Belief

Faith does not have to mean religion. For some, faith is spiritual devotion. For others, it is trust in life, commitment to truth, connection to meaning, confidence in the goodness of love, or a steady loyalty to values that do not change with circumstances.

In whatever form it takes, faith becomes an anchor. Because without an anchor, identity becomes vulnerable to every shifting opinion, outcome, or failure. We become dependent on external validation to tell us who we are. And external validation is unstable by nature.

A grounding belief system—spiritual, relational, philosophical, or values-based—changes the way you interpret yourself. It shifts the question from:

Who do others say I am?

to

Who am I at my core?

When my confidence has been shaken, returning to what I believe about human worth has helped me find my center again. That belief becomes a steadier voice than fear. It reminds me that insecurity is not a prophecy—it is a signal. It is something to tend, not something to obey.

For those who believe in God, this anchoring can feel even more personal. Because rooted worth is not just an idea—it is a relationship. It is hearing, again and again, the voice that speaks identity without shame:

> You are Mine.

> You are known.

> You are not disposable.

> You are not forgotten.

And even for those who use a different language, the concept remains: worth is not a moving target. It is a truth you return to. A home base. A steady ground beneath the shifting weather of emotion and circumstance.

When Worth Becomes Performance

Performance-based worth is exhausting because it has no finish line.

> If worth depends on success, you are only as valuable as your last win.

> If worth depends on approval, you are only as safe as your last interaction.

> If worth depends on productivity, you are only as worthy as your last output.

Performance-based worth breeds perfectionism. And perfectionism breeds fear. It creates a life where mistakes feel dangerous, and rest feels irresponsible. It trains the nervous system to stay hypervigilant—constantly scanning for what might disqualify you from love.

It also makes relationships transactional, because if you are trying to earn worth, you may begin to measure people the same way—what they give, what they produce, how they perform. Even if you never say it out loud, the internal scorekeeping creates distance.

Healthy identity grows from connection—not constant evaluation.

> **Connection to self:** being honest about needs, emotions, limits, desires.

> **Connection to others:** receiving and giving love without earning it.

> **Connection to truth:** returning to what is real, not what is fearful.

> **Connection to meaning:** remembering you are part of something larger than your performance.

Rooted worth comes from being, not proving.

I used to believe I was more valuable when I did everything right, when I was helpful, when I was impressive, when I was composed. But my deepest growth happened when I allowed myself to be imperfect and still worthy, when I stopped treating my humanity like a flaw.

When you live *from* worth instead of *for* worth, you do not become careless. You become free.

Words That Heal: Texts, Truths, and Declarations

Words shape identity.

We become what we repeatedly agree with.

This is why grounding texts and truths matter so much. Whether those truths come from Scripture, sacred writings, philosophy, psychology, poetry, or personal declarations, language can interrupt harmful narratives and rewrite inner foundations.

Truth does not just inform the mind. It heals the mind. But truth only heals when it moves from something we read to something we practice believing. That shift takes repetition. It takes intention. It takes choosing truth in moments when the old story is loud.

When self-doubt rises, many of us instinctively search for external reassurance—someone to affirm us, someone to validate us, someone to tell us we are okay. And reassurance can be helpful. But it is not stable if it is the only source of worth.

Grounding truth is different. It is internal. It is portable.

When I start feeling unworthy, I return to words that remind me I matter simply because I exist. Repeating that truth grounds me more than external reassurance ever could. It reorients me. It reminds my nervous system that I am not in danger because I am not perfect.

This is not denial. It is alignment.

Truth does not pretend everything is fine.

Truth says: You are still worthy while you heal.

Living From Worth Changes How You Love

When you live *from* worth instead of *for* worth, relationships become less transactional.

You stop using people as mirrors to confirm your value. You stop chasing approval as a substitute for belonging. You stop shrinking to be liked or performing to be chosen.

You become freer to love, and you become free to set boundaries.

Boundaries are not punishments. They are the natural behavior of a person who knows they matter. When you believe your worth is secure, you do not have to tolerate mistreatment to stay connected. You do not have to betray yourself to avoid conflict. You can love without losing yourself. You can give from fullness instead of from a place of lack.

Once I stopped chasing approval, I was able to show up more authentically. Knowing my worth is steady allows me to love others without becoming dependent on their response. I can be kind without overextending. I can be honest without fear. I can forgive without abandoning my limits.

Rooted worth overflows into consistency.

> When you are not trying to earn love, you can actually receive it.
>
> When you are not trying to prove your value, you can relax into connection.
>
> When you are not obsessed with being enough, you can finally be present.

Belovedness is not only a personal truth, but it also becomes a relational healing, because when you know you are valued, you stop treating yourself and others like projects. You begin relating from dignity.

Journal Prompt:

"What does being inherently valued mean for how I live?"

Write down three truths, affirmations, or beliefs that remind you of your worth.

Turn each one into a personal declaration, such as:

• "My worth is not dependent on my performance."

• "I am allowed to take up space."

• "I am valued even when I rest."

Closing Affirmation:

"I am not defined by what I do, but by who I am. My worth is inherent, secure, and unshaken. I am rooted, worthy, and free.

Chapter 10 — Body Image & Self-Talk: Shifting from Criticism to Compassion

Most of us learned to judge our bodies long before we learned to listen to them.

We learned it in mirrors.

In comments made casually but remembered vividly.

In clothing sizes.

In locker rooms.

In sermons, magazines, advertisements, and before-and-after photos.

And slowly, the body stopped being something we inhabited and became something we evaluated.

For many people, the inner conversation about the body is one of the harshest dialogues they live with every day. It speaks in comparisons. It catalogs flaws. It critiques without mercy. It treats the body like a problem to solve instead of a home to care for.

But the way you speak to your body matters.

Your body is listening.

This chapter is not about pretending you love every part of your body overnight. It is not about toxic positivity or ignoring real struggles with health, pain, or change. It is about shifting the tone of the relationship. It is about learning how to move from criticism to compassion—because healing does not grow in hostile environments.

The Language We Use With Our Bodies

The words you speak to and about your body reveal what you believe about your worth.

If the language is harsh, the belief underneath is often shame.

If the language is impatient, the belief underneath is control.

If the language is dismissive, the belief underneath is disconnection.

Criticism keeps us locked in cycles of striving and self-rejection. Compassion creates space for healing and alignment. One tightens the nervous system; the other softens it.

For years, my relationship with my body was transactional. I evaluated it based on how well it met expectations—my own and others'. I looked in the mirror and mentally listed everything I wanted to change. My body felt like a verdict: pass or fail.

What shifted was not my appearance, but my posture toward myself.

I began thanking my body for what it did: breathing, digesting, healing, carrying me through grief, stress, joy, and survival. Before, I only judged how it looked. That simple practice changed the entire conversation. The mirror became less of a battleground and more of a meeting place.

Our bodies are not projects to perfect.

They are temples to honor and care for.

Where Body Standards and Inner Critics Come From

Body criticism is rarely self-generated.

It is inherited.

It stems from cultural ideals that narrow the definition of beauty to impossible standards. From family comments spoken without awareness. From medical conversations that focus only on weight instead of wellness. From faith spaces that sometimes disconnect the spiritual from the physical. From comparisons that train the eye to look for lack rather than uniqueness.

Many of us learned to monitor our bodies because we learned that appearance affected safety, acceptance, or belonging. So, the inner critic stepped in as a form of protection: If I criticize myself first, maybe I won't be caught off guard.

But that voice did not originate in truth.

It originated in fear.

Once I recognized that most of my body shame did not come from me—but from what I absorbed growing up—I felt something loosen. Awareness gave me a choice. I could decide whether to keep carrying beliefs that were never aligned with compassion or truth.

You are allowed to unlearn standards that harm you.

You are allowed to reject messages that reduce your worth to a shape, size, or number.

Faith, the Body, and Sacred Stewardship

For those who come from a faith framework, body image often carries extra layers—sometimes healing, sometimes harm.

Scripture describes the body as a dwelling place of God's Spirit. Sacred. Purposeful. Worthy of care. That language is not meant to shame the body into compliance—it is meant to restore dignity.

To see the body as a temple is not to obsess over it.

It is to steward it.

Stewardship is different from control.

Control punishes. Stewardship listens.

Control demands. Stewardship cooperates.

When I began seeing my body as a vessel instead of a verdict, everything changed. I stopped treating it like something to dominate and started treating it like something to partner with. Nourishment replaced restriction. Rest replaced punishment. Gratitude replaced resentment.

Even for those who use different spiritual language, the principle remains: the body is part of creation, not separate from it. It is not an obstacle to spirituality; it is an expression of it.

When we reconnect body and spirit, compassion becomes natural.

Self-Talk as a Healing Practice

Your inner dialogue shapes your nervous system.

Words can reinforce lies or speak the truth. They can tighten the body or relax it. They can deepen shame or open pathways to peace.

Changing self-talk does not start with forcing positivity. It begins with awareness. By catching the script before it takes root. By noticing how a sentence lands in the body.

When a thought creates tension, contraction, or despair, it is likely not the truth. Truth may be challenging, but it does not dehumanize. It corrects without contempt.

One of the most powerful shifts I made was replacing "I hate this about me" with "I'm learning to love this part of me." That sentence did not deny struggle. It allowed growth. And over time, it changed not only how I looked at myself, but how I lived.

Compassionate self-talk is not indulgent.

It is neurologically and emotionally reparative.

Gratitude as the Foundation of Healing

Gratitude does not mean settling.

It means acknowledging reality without hostility.

Gratitude grounds us in the present moment. It redirects attention from what is missing to what is working. It allows appreciation to coexist with the desire for growth.

Simple acts—stretching, breathing deeply, resting, eating mindfully—become sacred when done with thankfulness. They signal to the body that it is safe, valued, and respected.

I once believed gratitude meant giving up. Now I see it as a celebration. Thanking my body daily reminds me that my worth does not depend on perfection—my worth is already present.

Healing body image does not begin with alteration.

It begins with appreciation.

Journal Prompt:

"How can I speak life over my body?"

Write a letter to your body, thanking it for its strength, resilience, and the life it allows you to live. Replace every self-criticism with a truth statement of compassion.

End with this affirmation:

"My body is a good gift. I release judgment and choose gratitude. I speak life, love, and truth over the body that carries my soul."

Chapter 11 — Failure as Teacher, Not Title: Reframing Mistakes as Growth

Failure is a word most of us learned to fear before we ever learned to define it.

We heard it in classrooms where grades felt like identity.

We felt it in family systems where mistakes were punished instead of guided.

We carried it into adulthood, where success became a currency for belonging.

And somewhere along the way, many of us stopped seeing failure as an experience and started treating it like a verdict.

As if one setback could name us.

As if one wrong turn could erase us.

As if one collapse meant we were now permanently disqualified.

But failure was never meant to be a title.

Failure is an event.

A moment.

A misstep.

A lesson in progress.

And if you have been using failure as proof that something is wrong with you, I want to offer a different possibility:

What if failure is not the end of your story… but part of its formation?

What if failure is not a wall… but a doorway?

This chapter is about learning how to reinterpret falling short. It is about separating your identity from outcomes, allowing grace to shape your inner voice, and letting mistakes become momentum instead of shame.

Because you are not your worst moment.

You are the person learning through it.

When You Hear "Failure," What Rises Up?

Failure can trigger different emotions depending on what you were taught it meant.

For some people, failure means danger. It activates fear and urgency, because falling short once may have cost them love, belonging, or safety.

For others, failure means shame. A hot, sinking feeling that says: I am not good enough. Shame does not just point to what went wrong. It points at you.

For others, failure feels motivating—like a challenge to overcome, a problem to solve, a chance to redeem themselves quickly.

But no matter the emotional response, the deeper question is often the same:

What do I believe failure says about me?

Because that belief becomes your reality.

Culture tends to frame failure as an ending. It celebrates success like a reward for being worthy and treats mistakes like proof of being less. But life does not work that way. Most growth is messy. Most learning is imperfect. Most becoming is built on trial and error and refinement.

Failure is feedback.

> It shows you what didn't work.

> It reveals what needs attention.

> It exposes what you still need to learn.

> It invites humility.

> It forms resilience.

I used to fear failure more than anything. I avoided risks that mattered because I could not bear the idea of being wrong. But over time, I began to see failure differently—not as final, but as formative, not as proof of inadequacy, but as information. Failure started showing me where I could grow.

And that shift in perspective changed everything.

Separating Identity From Outcome

There is a subtle but powerful difference between saying:

"I failed."

and

"I am a failure."

One describes an experience. The other assigns an identity.

Many of us collapse those two sentences into one without realizing it. And when we tie identity to success, risk becomes terrifying. We avoid trying because we cannot afford to be wrong. We stay small because expansion would require learning. We cling to perfectionism because we believe it is protection.

But resilient people understand something important:

Failure is data, not a definition.

A result is not a name.

An outcome is not a verdict.

A setback is not a prophecy.

You are not your results—you are the person learning through them.

When a project didn't succeed, I used to take it personally. I would spiral into self-judgment and ask, "What's wrong with me?" But now I ask, "What did this teach me?" That question creates movement instead of collapse.

It turns regret into reflection.

It turns shame into wisdom.

It turns failure into formation.

Separating identity from outcome is not denial. It is truth. It is remembering that your value does not rise and fall with your achievements.

Your worth is not a scoreboard.

Faith and Falling Short: The Grace Story

If you come from faith, Scripture offers a radically different relationship with failure than culture does.

The Bible is full of imperfect people who fell short—sometimes publicly, sometimes painfully—yet their failures were not the end of their calling. They were a part of their shaping.

Moses struggled with fear and anger. David made devastating choices. Elijah collapsed under exhaustion. Jonah ran. Peter denied the One he loved. And yet, redemption still wrote the larger story.

Faith teaches that failure is not disqualification.

God uses failure to shape character, humility, and dependence—not to crush a person into shame. Grace does not pretend that mistakes do not matter. Grace says mistakes are not stronger than mercy. Grace holds both truth and restoration.

Peter's story comforts me deeply. He denied Yeshua—not once, but three times. That is not a small failure. That is betrayal born from fear. Yet he was restored. Still called. Still trusted. Still used.

That reminds me that failure is not the end.

It can be preparation.

Grace turns failure into formation and reminds us that nothing is wasted when brought into truth. Even our missteps can become sacred teachers.

Turning Mistakes Into Momentum

Failure becomes powerful when we do something with it.

> Not by punishing ourselves.

> Not by pretending it didn't happen.

> Not by rewriting history.

But by reflecting, adjusting, and moving forward.

One of the

 most healing shifts is learning to ask different questions after a setback.

Instead of: "How could I be so stupid?"

Ask: "What was I needing in that moment?"

Instead of: "I ruined everything."

Ask: "What did I learn, and what's the next step?"

Instead of: "This proves I'm not cut out for this."

Ask: "What support or skill do I need to grow?"

Transformation happens when lessons replace labels.

After a relationship failed, I used to rush to replace it—trying to prove I was still lovable, still wanted, still okay. But eventually I chose a different response. I paused. I reflected. I asked what the relationship revealed about my patterns, my needs, and my boundaries. That pause taught me what I needed to heal before moving forward.

That is momentum. Not rushing forward to outrun pain—but walking forward with wisdom.

Grace: The Antidote to Shame

Grace is not indulgence.

Grace is clarity without cruelty.

Grace is the ability to see yourself honestly and still choose compassion. It does not erase responsibility—it transforms it into growth.

Grace says:

Yes, you fell short.

Yes, you made a mistake.

Yes, you have something to learn.

And no, this does not make you unworthy.

Failure does not mean "bad."

Failure means human.

When you practice grace, you can own your mistakes without being owned by them. You can apologize without self-destruction. You can reflect without spiraling. You can repair without collapsing.

Grace changed everything for me. Instead of saying "I blew it," I now say, "I learned from it." That shift turned shame into strength. It turned failure into a teacher instead of a judge.

And slowly, I learned to interpret setbacks as part of my becoming, not proof that I am broken. Because I am not my worst moment. I am the one, like the phoenix in the RISE logo, learning how to rise from the ashes.

Journal Prompt:

"What has failure taught me about who I am?"

List three experiences you once labeled as failures and write one lesson or strength each gave you. Then thank God for how He used them to grow you.

End with this affirmation:

"Failure is not my name—growth is. I am learning, evolving, and becoming who I was created to be through every fall and rise."

Chapter 12 — Community & Reflection: Seeing Yourself Through Healthy Connections

We do not discover who we are in isolation.

Even the most self-aware people need reflection. Not the kind found in mirrors or inner dialogue alone, but the kind that happens when another human being sees us clearly and speaks truth with care. Identity is formed internally, but it is revealed relationally.

Community is not optional to becoming whole—it is essential.

Healthy relationships act like mirrors. They reflect back what we cannot always see: our strengths, our growth, our blind spots, and our worth. When our inner voice becomes distorted by fear, shame, or exhaustion, community helps recalibrate the truth.

This chapter is about learning how to see yourself through healthy connections rather than harmful ones. It is about recognizing the difference between isolation and solitude, between accountability and control, between community that drains and community that restores.

Because the people you surround yourself with shape the way you see yourself.

The People Who Reflect Your True Self

There are people in your life who call you higher—not through pressure, but through presence. They speak truth without crushing you. They remind you who you are when you forget. They see beyond your fear and into your potential.

These are the people who reflect your true self.

A healthy community does not flatter. It does not manipulate. It does not demand that you turn into someone else to belong. Instead, it gently mirrors back what is already there—your courage, your compassion, your wisdom, your becoming.

Often, we discover parts of ourselves in relationships that we could never access alone. A friend names a strength you underestimated. A mentor sees leadership where you saw insecurity. A trusted voice reminds you of the truth when your inner critic grows loud.

I have a friend who speaks truth gently. When I start doubting myself, she reminds me who I am in God—not with sermons or pressure, but with steady presence. Her reflection has helped me see myself with more grace. Through her eyes, I learned how to soften my own.

Being seen this way is healing.

Because when someone reflects your worth back to you consistently, it becomes easier to believe it yourself.

The Cost of Isolation and Unhealthy Influence

While a healthy community clarifies identity, isolation distorts it.

Isolation is not the same as solitude. Solitude restores. Isolation isolates us from corrective truth. Isolation amplifies fear and allows shame to echo unchecked. When we withdraw completely—especially after being hurt—the inner narrative often becomes harsher, not quieter.

An unhealthy community can be just as damaging.

Toxic environments reinforce insecurity, competition, comparison, and conditional belonging. They reward performance instead of presence. They confuse criticism with accountability and control with care. Over time, these dynamics teach us to doubt ourselves, silence our needs, and question our worth.

When I isolated myself, my thoughts got louder and darker. I replayed my fears without interruption. Community brought light back in—not because others fixed me, but because their presence interrupted the lies. Healing was not meant to happen in hiding.

We are shaped by the voices we allow close.

Isolation may feel protective, but in the long term, it starves the soul of reflection and warmth. An unhealthy connection drains energy instead of restoring it. The question is not whether you need community, but what kind.

Growth Through Relational Reflection

One of the most uncomfortable—and transformative—roles the community plays is self-awareness.

Relationships reveal where we are still healing and where we have grown strong. They expose patterns we cannot see from the inside. When given with love, feedback becomes refinement rather than rejection.

God often speaks through people—not just to affirm us, but to gently challenge us.

Someone once pointed out that I avoid rest because I equate stillness with laziness. It stung—but they were right. That mirror moment changed how I treat myself. I realized how deeply productivity had shaped my identity, and how little permission I had given myself to simply be.

Correction spoken without love wounds. Truth spoken with love refines.

A healthy community offers both affirmation and challenge without shame. It helps us grow in humility without losing dignity. It invites us into deeper alignment, not conformity.

How we respond to feedback matters. Growth does not require defensiveness—it requires discernment. Not every voice deserves authority, but the right voices can become instruments of healing.

The Markers of Healthy Community

A healthy community feels different in the body.

It feels safe—not perfect, but secure.

It feels honest—not harsh.

It feels supportive—not suffocating.

A healthy community celebrates differences without competition. It does not require sameness to belong. It honors individual growth while protecting collective well-being.

Trust is present. Empathy is practiced. Boundaries are respected. Purpose is shared—not imposed.

A healthy community feels like a Sabbath for the soul. Peaceful. Restoring. Honest. A place where you can exhale without explanation.

It is where you can show up as you are—unfinished, imperfect, still learning—and remain loved.

These spaces do not avoid conflict, but they handle it with care. They allow space for growth without using fear as motivation. They model grace in action.

And importantly, a healthy community is mutual. It is not about being rescued or rescuing others. It is about walking alongside one another with integrity.

Building and Nurturing Life-Giving Connections

A healthy community does not happen by accident.

It is built through consistency, vulnerability, and intentional presence. It requires showing up even when it feels easier to retreat. It grows when we choose honesty over image and connection over convenience.

We cannot wait for the community to find us—we must also participate in creating it.

That might look like sending the text first. Asking real questions. Listening without fixing. Offering encouragement without agenda. Practicing reliability in small ways.

Reflection within the community deepens identity and empathy. When we allow others to see us and we choose to truly see them, connection becomes sacred.

I started checking in on friends regularly—not just when they needed help. Over time, those simple texts became sacred spaces of honesty and healing for both of us. The community did not feel dramatic or loud. It felt faithful.

When we bring God's presence into our interactions—through patience, kindness, humility, and truth—community becomes a place where identity is strengthened, not diminished.

Journal Prompt:

"Who mirrors back the truth of who I am?"

List three people who reflect your best qualities, and three ways you can intentionally reflect encouragement back to others.

End with this affirmation:

"I am shaped and strengthened through connection. In a healthy community, I see myself more clearly and love more freely."

About R.I.S.E.

R.I.S.E. was created as a place of encouragement, clarity, and support for those choosing a whole food plant-based lifestyle and seeking to live in whole-being wellness. It is a framework for living that honors the Creator's original design for the body, mind, and spirit.

R.I.S.E. means:

Rooted in Truth – grounded in unshakable principles rather than passing trends.

Intentional in Habits – choosing daily practices that nourish and strengthen both body and soul.

Strong in Spirit – cultivating inner resilience, emotional stability, and faith for life's challenges.

Energized for Life – experiencing vibrancy, joy, and well-being through alignment, simplicity, and purpose.

Through R.I.S.E., you'll discover tools, teachings, and community support that help you walk toward wholeness with confidence. It's not only about food—it's about restoring balance, reclaiming identity, living with intention, and stepping into the fullness of life you were created for.

Every resource connected to R.I.S.E., including this book and companion journal, is designed to equip, uplift, and inspire you as you grow in wellness and walk out your calling with clarity and courage.

Feel free to reach out anytime to learn more about R.I.S.E. using the QR code below.

About the Author

Angel Tate Keaton is the founder of Healthy in Heart Media and the creator of the RISE™ Rooted, Intentional, Strong, Energized, a Whole-Being Wellness Framework. As a trauma survivor, teacher, author, and guide, Angel writes from the intersections of faith, identity, emotional healing, and whole-being restoration. Her work invites others to remember who they are beneath the labels, lies, and lifetimes of survival—and to step into the truth of who they were created to become.

After decades of healing work, Angel discovered that transformation doesn't begin with performance, perfection, or self-improvement—it starts with identity. This book and companion journal reflect her heart: to help others move from wounded stories to whole stories, from exhaustion to alignment, and from fractured self-image to beloved self-understanding. Through simple prompts, gentle questions, and the RISE rhythm of weekly reflection, she guides readers into a deeper clarity with a grounded confidence.

Angel believes that every person carries divine worth and that healing unfolds not by running faster but by returning to truth. Her mission is to create resources that help individuals rebuild their identity, release shame, reclaim resilience, and rise with purpose—spiritually, emotionally, and physically. Through books, journals, guides, community circles, and teaching, she is dedicated to equipping others to live lives that are rooted in truth, intentional in purpose, strong in identity, and energized in spirit.

Angel lives in Virginia with her husband, Todd, and their daughter, where they continue to write, teach, and walk out whole-being living with a shared passion for helping others rediscover the path back to themselves—and back to the One who made them.

Mission of Healthy in Heart

Healthy in Heart Media, LLC exists to help people return to wholeness—body, mind, and spirit—through Hebraic truth, Eden-aligned living, and compassionate, practical tools.

We:

- Publish books, journals, devotionals, and children's resources that make spiritual formation simple and doable.
- Guide households into oil-free, whole-food, plant-based eating through meal plans, prep systems, and gentle re-entry guides.
- Cultivate Sabbath and seasonal practices that restore pace, presence, and peace.

Mission in one line:

To restore shalom in real lives through truth, tools, and tables—so homes and communities become a little piece of Eden.

Join the Healthy in Heart Community

Wholeness is not a journey we walk alone. If this book has strengthened your spirit, I invite you to stay connected with a community that is growing, learning, and returning to whole-being wellness together.

Visit the Healthy in Heart Website

Find more books, journals, recipes, botanical resources, and tools for whole-being wellness.

Website: HealthyInHeart.com

Follow Along on Social Media

Receive weekly encouragement, recipe ideas, spiritual reflections, and behind-the-scenes updates on upcoming projects.

YouTube | Instagram| Facebook

@healthyinheart

Pinterest

@healthyinheart1

Join the Sabbath Table Gathering

A weekly space of peace, Scripture, reflection, shared learning, and social connection.

We gather to slow down, honor the rhythm God built into creation, and get to know one another. We talk about whatever subject comes up.

Everyone is welcome — whether you're exploring Sabbath for the first time or restoring it in your home. To request an invite:

https://healthyinheart.com/contact-me-about-our-sabbath-table-gathering

The RISE™ Momentum Circle

If you desire deeper transformation, the RISE Circle offers guided group discussion rooted in whole-being wellness:

Rooted • Intentional • Strong • Energized

Together we grow in identity, emotional strength, nourishing rhythms, and whole-being wellness.

We meet on Zoom on Thursdays from 5:00 PM to 6:30 PM. To request an invite:

https://healthyinheart.com/contact-me-about-r-i-s-e

Stay Connected

Subscribe to the Healthy in Heart newsletter email list for free resources, new recipes, devotional content, early book releases, and special community invitations.

https://healthyinheart.com/subscribe

You don't have to walk toward wholeness alone.

Join us — and step into a community shaped by truth, simplicity, joy, and shalom.

Explore More

Your journey doesn't have to end here. If these pages have spoken to you, I'd love to walk further with you. My online store is filled with resources created to nourish your identity, strengthen your spirit, and support whole-being wellness—books that deepen your walk, journals that guide your reflection, themed shirts and home goods that encourage you daily, and handmade items crafted with prayer and purpose.

Every product is designed to remind you of who you are and Who walks with you. Come see what's waiting for you at **HealthyInHeart.com**

Shop Healthy in Heart Store

Each week, I release new blog articles and plant-based recipes designed to support your health, healing, identity, and whole-being wellness. From emotional and spiritual encouragement to practical nourishment for your body, these writings are meant to walk with you—one small step at a time.

You'll find teachings on R.I.S.E. principles, identity and worth, emotional healing, Hebraic roots, and simple homemade recipes that help you thrive.

Join me at HealthyInHeart.com for weekly encouragement, truth, and nourishment for both body and soul. Subscribe to my newsletter by following this QR code where you can keep up-to-date on my most recent posts, new books, and monthly updates.

Sign up for the Newsletter!

The Healthy in Heart Library

The Daniel Fast 21-Day Meal Plan: Simple Plant-Based Nourishment for Mind, Body, & Spirit Eat Well. Pray Deep. Stand Strong.

Books in the Series

Book 1- *The Eden Way*™*: Reclaiming Body, Mind, and Spirit Through the Creator's Original Design*

Book 2 -*The Eden Way*™ *Journal: 49-Days to Reset Body, Mind, and Spirit* (Companion to Book 1)

Books in the Series

The Little Keepers of the Garden™*: Seeds of Truth Collection*

Seeds of Truth Activity Book: The Little Keepers of the Garden™ *Series*

Books in the Series

RISE™ Wellness Journal—Rooted, Intentional, Strong, Energized: Embrace One Year of Habits, Healing, and Hope

RISE™ The Beginning of Balance—How Rooted, Intentional, Strong, and Energized Living Transforms the Whole Self: A Framework for Whole-Being Wellness

The Beginning of Balance Chronicles: The Lived Record of Learning to Inhabit RISE™

The RISE™ Circle of Wholeness Collection

Identity & Worth Volume 1

RISE™ Identity & Worth Living a Rooted, Intentional, Strong, and Energized Life—Volume 1

RISE™ Identity & Worth Journal: A 12-Week Journey to a Rooted, Intentional, Strong, and Energized Life—Volume 1 (Companion to Identity & Worth, Volume 1)

Explore all titles and resources at HealthyInHeart.com

If This Book Spoke to You…

A Note from the Author

If this journey has nourished your body, quieted old patterns, renewed your mind, or gently drawn you closer to God through simplicity and intention, thank you for walking it with me.

Books like this find their way into the right hands not through algorithms alone, but through shared stories. When readers take a moment to reflect publicly—whether in a few sentences or a single honest thought—it becomes a signpost for someone else who is searching for the same clarity, healing, or rest.

Your words matter more than you know.

They help others recognize themselves in this path.

They remind someone that restoration is possible.

If you feel led, I would be deeply grateful if you shared a brief review wherever you normally discover books—Amazon, Goodreads, or HealthyInHeart.com.

Thank you for choosing nourishment over noise, truth over striving, and faithfulness over perfection.

And thank you for helping this message reach those who are longing to return to what is whole.

With gratitude,

Angel Tate Keaton

www.ingramcontent.com/pod-product-compliance
Lightning Source LLC
Chambersburg PA
CBHW081718120626
46550CB00010B/3167